Scotl

Edwin Moore spent eighteen years working in non-fiction publishing. He is also the author of several books, including *Lemmings Don't Leap: 180 Myths, Misconceptions and Urban Legends Exploded* (2006), *Brief Encounters: Meetings between (mostly) Remarkable People* (2007) and the *Everyman Guide to Edinburgh*. He wrote obituaries for *The Times* (2004–14), tweets at EdwinMoore@ GlasgowAlbum and blogs at http://glasgowalbum.blogspot. co.uk. The blog (which has become quite popular with Glaswegians home and abroad) focuses on what can be seen on walks and cycles within an ever-changing Glasgow, from the ongoing destruction of inconvenient buildings to festivals such as the Mela.

'Entertaining and scholarly – he writes like a Scottish Bill Bryson' *Dundee Courier*

'Moore proceeds from a sincere and controversial first principle: Scotland is really a rather pleasant and interesting place… As a work of popular scholarship it's in a different league' *Sunday Times*

'Well-crafted and witty' *Aberdeen Press and Journal*

'A fascinating look at the history of Scotland… Edwin Moore has collected a thousand important facts about this beautiful country, covering Scottish history and culture, correcting misconceptions, and examining the mysteries of haggis and bagpipes with insight, warmth and impressive attention to detail.' *Good Book Guide*

'A recipe for revealing how horribly ill informed you are about your country… Oh so addictive' *i-on Glasgow*

'Edwin celebrates all that sets us Scots as a race apart – our language, law, flora, food, and of course, our people. From our poets, architects and inventors, to our artists, entertainers and fighters. But he doesn't shy away from the more unpleasant aspects of our history.' *Sunday Post*

'We think we know all about William Wallace, Robert the Bruce and the Union of the Crowns. However, according to Edwin Moore, we're still in the dark about many aspects of our history and culture' *The Big Issue*

'Despite its apparently humorous format, this is a serious and extensive dictionary on all things Scottish; from Jean Redpath to Lorne sausage, from Flodden to the Corries. Is particularly good on history and minutiae. There's a useful chapter on famous Scottish legal cases and another on literature. Excellent.' Royal Scottish Legion

'A real treat for the serendipitous Scotophile' Reginald Hill

SCOTLAND

1,001 Things You Need to Know

Edwin Moore

Atlantic Books
LONDON

First published in hardback in Great Britain in 2008
by Atlantic Books, an imprint of Atlantic Books Ltd.

This revised paperback edition published in Great Britain
in 2016 by Atlantic Books

1 3 5 7 9 10 8 6 4 2

A CIP catalogue record for this book is available
from the British Library.

Paperback ISBN: 9781782395874
E-book ISBN: 9780857899330

Printed in Great Britain by Clays Ltd, St Ives plc

Atlantic Books
An imprint of Atlantic Books Ltd
Ormond House
26–27 Boswell Street
London WCIN 3JZ

Contents

Preface to the 2016 edition

❖

'Stands Scotland where it did?' A very good question there, MacDuff, but answering it in full is mibbe a wee bit beyond the scope of this book, which has been updated to include details of both the 2015 Referendum and the 2016 Holyrood election, with other necessary amendments and revisions. Post-Referendum Scotland is a land of many opinions, and not just the simple binary one of 'Yes' or 'No' to independence.

Scotland has always been a contrary sort of place. Jacobite Scotland and Covenanter Scotland are both part of what we are, yet neither is – to say the least – quite comfortable with the other: we have democratic traditions, we also have authoritarian traditions, and time adds fresh threads to the national tartan.

We are a patchwork of peoples, beliefs and traditions: as Robert Louis Stevenson said, 'Scotland is indefinable… it has no unity except upon the map'. We have doom and gloom and prejudice in our national mix; we also have a heritage of Enlightenment, innovation and literature that has shaped the modern world, as I hope this book shows. And we also like to laugh from time to time, if not always at ourselves. It is a fascinating time to be a Scot. And to celebrate the Scotland of Chic Murray, Robert Adam, Billy Connolly, Lulu, Bert Jansch, Archie Gemmil, Dundee United beating Barcelona home and away, Billy McNeill, John Brown and Alex McLeish,

Andy Murray, the Glasgow Boys, the Glasgow Girls, James Macmillan, Flora MacDonald, Colin Mackenzie restoring India's Buddhist history, Robert Louis Stevenson (and Robert Stevenson), Robert Burns, the Great Highland Bagpipe, the Forth Rail Bridge, the Tay Rail Bridge, William McGonagall, the brochs, Thomas Telford, Thomas the Rhymer, Annie Lennox, Ivor Cutler, the Border Ballads, Sir Walter Scott, Sir Colin 'Slowcoach' Campbell, Alexander Greek Thomson, David Hume, Adam Smith, George Wyllie, and the new, often unsettling voices such as the rapper Loki and the Kartel, and the geniuses behind *Still Game*, Greg Hemphill and Ford Kiernan – Scotland's real heritage. It's a lot to be proud of.

Acknowledgements

❖

I must first of all thank my editor, Sarah Castleton, and my copy editor, Morag Lyall, for their intelligence, knowledge, common sense and tact. They have saved me from many pitfalls and pratfalls; thanks again, guys. The responsibility and blame for any remaining errors rest with the author, who was once (unfairly!) pilloried in the Scottish media for a book that missed out the Battle of Bannockburn. I have checked and double-checked and Bannockburn is here at least once, though no doubt other things are missing.

Many thanks also to: our eldest daughter Helen Moore for research; Alice Goldie ditto; Bruce Whyte, Morag and Alisdair Law, and Fiona Moore for Gaelic input, our youngest daughter Rowan Moore for Gaelic spelling; Jude Stewart and Alex Cochrane for useful tips; Alex Adamson of Scottish Civic Trust for advice on endangered buildings; and lastly Mike Munro, poet and patter merchant extraordinaire – thanks again, Mike.

2016 Edition
Many thanks to James Nightingale, editor of this edition, for his advice and support, and to Laura Booth for proofreading the revised text.

This book is for my late brother Colin and for my sister Jean, and (again) for our late mother, who worked her socks off to feed and clothe her family and hated nobody, and who was so Scottish she was known to put her finger on the ball during televised England–Scotland games to pull it back into the England half. It never worked, alas.

1

PEOPLE AND PLACES

❖❖❖

—— The Origin of Scotland ——

The land we call 'Scotland' was originally not part of what we call 'Britain' – indeed it wasn't even part of Europe, but part of the ancient continent of Laurentia, along with most of what we now call 'North America'. We even share our types of dinosaurs with North America rather than Europe.

The first union between 'England' and 'Scotland' took place around 400 million years ago with the Caledonian Orogeny, when a great collision of continents joined us together and created mountains the size of the Alps in Scotland. Then, 60 million years ago, the Atlantic swept between Scotland and North America, sundering the old conjoined regions for ever. It was a Scot, James Hutton (see p. 120), who first worked out that the rocks in Scotland demonstrated that the earth must be very old indeed.

We were left with a Scotland which the 1911 *Encylopaedia Britannica* describes as 'divided into three geographical regions – the "Highlands" (subdivided by Glen More into the North-Western and South-Eastern Highlands); the Central Plain or "Lowlands" (a tract of south-westerly to north-easterly trend, between a line drawn roughly from Girvan to Dunbar and a line drawn from Dumbarton to Stonehaven); and the "Southern Uplands"'.

The Hebrides may be regarded as distinct from the rest of the Highlands, and Orkney and Shetland are a different matter altogether. However defined, the various Scottish regions have – by universal consent – some of the finest landscapes in the world: hills, glens and lochs that are both accessible and (if you are sensible) safe. You can be having breakfast in a top-class hotel in Glasgow at 9 a.m. and by noon be trekking up the Lost Valley in Glencoe, in the footsteps of Highland rustlers.

—— Ten Great Lochs ——

Safety note: the depths recorded here are maximum depths. Swimmers should take note that although these lochs may look inviting in summer, the water will be cold and the currents are dangerous: Loch Lomond in particular has swallowed many an unwary swimmer.

LAKE OF MENTEITH (a wee loch)
A very pretty Perthshire loch, just 13 miles from Stirling. The Lake of Menteith is often said to be the only 'lake' in Scotland, which is not true, but it is certainly the best known in that very small category. The name derives from 'laich' which is an old Lallans word meaning 'low'. The loch has a few islets, on one of which is Inchmahome Priory, which sheltered the four-year-old Mary, Queen of Scots in 1547.

LOCH AWE (25½ miles long, 305 feet deep, but mostly much shallower)
Scotland's longest loch has huge trout (the British record brownie of 31 pounds was caught here) and pike.

LOCH CORUISK (over 4 miles long)
Loch Coruisk nestles under the Skye Cuillins and is quite

possibly the most dramatically sited patch of fresh water in the world. The River Coruisk which runs into the sea here is 400 yards long: one of the shortest rivers in Britain.

LOCH KATRINE *(8 miles long, over half a mile wide)*
A highly romantic loch that has a vital utilitarian function, supplying vast quantities of water to Glasgow and its environs along a 26-mile aqueduct built in 1855. The loch is the setting for Sir Walter Scott's poem 'The Lady of the Lake' (1810) and became a major tourist attraction as a result.

LOCH LAGAN *(a very wee loch)*
A tiny loch this, a lochan really, sited in Coire Lagan on Skye, and surrounded by the Cuillins. Many a climber has refreshed themselves in this loch, which can easily be reached (with just a bit of hand as well as foot work) from the Glen Brittle campsite for a Tolkienesque picnic.

LOCH LOMOND *(24 miles long, 623 feet deep)*
The eastern side of the loch is dominated by Ben Lomond. The loch area is a naturalist's paradise: home to around 25 per cent of all recorded wild plants in Britain, around 200 species of birds have been found here. And all this is just a few miles from Glasgow. The origin of the haunting song 'Loch Lomond' is unknown, although there is a tradition that it was written by a Jacobite prisoner awaiting execution (the 'low road' is the path taken by the dead).

> Oh, ye'll tak' the high road, and I'll tak' the low road,
> And I'll be in Scotland afore ye;
> But me and my true love will never meet again
> On the bonnie, bonnie banks o' Loch Lomond.

Loch Morar (12 miles long, 1,017 feet deep)

It would be possible to stand the Eiffel Tower in Loch Morar's deepest point with 30 feet to spare. It is the deepest lake in Britain, and a good bit deeper than the sea around Britain.

Loch Ness (23 miles long, 754 feet deep)

Loch Ness is an extraordinary great basin of water – by far the largest volume of water of any Scottish loch at over 263,000 cubic feet. The BT Tower in London could stand up in it with 130 feet to spare, and it contains more water than every English and Welsh lake combined. The loch links Fort William and Inverness through the Caledonian Canal.

Loch Shiel (17 miles long, 400 feet deep)

A long loch surrounded by beautiful, lonely hills. The 1745 Rebellion began on this loch: Bonnie Prince Charlie was rowed its length to Glenfinnan, where his standard was raised.

Loch Tay (14 miles long, 500 feet deep)

The largest loch in Perthshire. There have been settlements around Loch Tay since the Iron Age, indeed settlements on the loch itself, in the form of 'crannogs', a Scottish and Irish loch dwelling. There is a reconstruction of one on the loch.

—— Five Great Glens ——

Glen Affric

Glen Affric is a Caledonian Forest Reserve, and is home to many of Scotland's rarest animals, including red squirrels, pine martens and crossbills. The Caledonian pine wood here is one of the largest in Scotland.

GLENCOE

Glencoe is a magnificent glen, hemmed in by sublimely picturesque mountains on both sides. Dorothy Wordsworth wrote a very fine description of Glencoe in her 1893 journal, but ended by confessing to feeling a trifle let down: 'we had been prepared for images of terror... The place had nothing of this character, the glen being open to the eye of day, the mountains retiring in independent majesty.' The reason for this view of Glencoe as a place of 'terror' is of course the Glencoe Massacre and the mistaken belief that the name means 'Glen of Weeping' (it may mean 'narrow glen' but is likely named after the River Coe). Some enthusiasts over-compensate for this misunderstanding by describing Glencoe as quite a jolly place, but it can be gloomy enough in the rain.

GLENEAGLES

Gleneagles is a pretty valley running through the Ochil Hills. The old attractions of the glen (formerly owned by the Haldanes) include a (largely rebuilt) twelfth-century chapel and a ruined castle, but the place has become synonymous now with the internationally renowned Gleneagles Hotel at Auchterarder, scene also of many a summit, most notably the G8 Summit of 2005. The name Gleneagles has nothing to do with eagles, and probably derives from the Gaelic for 'church'.

GLEN LYON

Glen Lyon stretches for 25 miles from Loch Lyon to Fortingall, and is arguably the least well-known of Scotland's great glens. The land is fertile, highly desirable, and is laden with history. 'Mad Colin' Campbell built Meggernie Castle here in the 1580s: Mad Colin had a short way with thieves, once hanging thirty MacDonald raiders in one go.

THE GREAT GLEN

The Great Glen stretches for over 70 miles between Fort William and Inverness, a route of historically strategic importance. It is a series of valleys following the Great Glen Fault: the Caledonian Canal runs through here, linking rivers and lochs into one great watery thoroughfare, from Loch Linnhe in the west right through to the River Ness. The Great Glen Way was opened in 2002.

—— Nine Great Mountains and Hills ——

These hills are all serious lumps of rock: they demand good hillwalking equipment and preparation if you want to ascend them. I have a long defunct guidebook to Skye which recommends that families should take hampers up to the top of Sgurr nan Gillean – no, no, you shouldn't. Ascents can be tricky even in the summer; spring and autumn require real care, and forget about winter unless you are experienced in winter climbing. Mountains over 3,000 feet are called Munros and those who collect ascents of them are called Munro-baggers; mountains over 2,500 feet but below Munro status are called Corbetts.

BEN CRUACHAN (3,689 feet)

Cruachan towers above Loch Awe and is easy to ascend. The hill is mentioned in John Barbour's epic poem *The Brus* (*c*.1376), where it is reckoned to be the highest peak in Britain:

> I trow that nocht in all Bretane
> Ane hear [higher] hill may fundin be.

The poem describes a battle between Bruce's men and the MacDougalls, and if you looked down at the loch that day in

1307 you would have seen Bruce's war galleys beaching below you. Both Wordsworth and Scott also praised this shapely hill. This was Campbell country, and 'Cruachan!' was the war cry of the Campbells.

BEN LOMOND *(3,196 feet)*
The most southerly of the Munros and the most accessible from a city: just a short drive from Glasgow brings you to a well-maintained path at Rowardennan which will lead you (after about three hours) to a fine Highland summit. The view of Loch Lomond is wonderful. Unlike many Scottish hills, the descent from Ben Lomond is easy-going.

BEN MACDHUI *(4,295 feet)*
This is Britain's second-highest mountain, and many a walker and climber has ended up battling down the slopes, in the dying light, against the elements. Ben MacDhui is haunted by a spectral figure called 'the Big Grey Man'. Rationalist spoil-sports say this is a trick of the light (a 'brocken spectre'); others 'feel' something they claim not to feel on other hills, and often something not quite friendly… Just don't panic – this is not a place to lose your judgement.

BEN NEVIS *(4,408 feet)*
The highest mountain in Britain rises from sea level to what can be an arctic environment in winter. There is a well-worn tourist track up the mountain, and thousands of visitors go up every summer. The average temperature at the summit is one degree below freezing, and the view is magnificent if you are there on the one out of ten days it is clear. There are climbing routes on the mountain that have claimed lives over the years, but walkers can die just as easily here by veering off the path.

The first recorded ascent was in 1771, and an observatory (now ruined) was built there in 1883. There have been many odd ascents: a brave Ford agent drove a Model T Ford to the summit in 1911; Glasgow University students took a bed up in 1981; and in 2008, a group of disabled people were pushed to the top in their wheelchairs.

BEN VRACKIE (2,757 feet)
A great walk and a great view at the top. You can climb this hill from either Killiecrankie or Pitlochry. It's an easy ascent, and you can see for miles and miles on a good day. NB: if you come up from Pitlochry, save time for a look at the village of Moulin and its splendid Victorian church. Many ancient paths crossed here at Moulin, a town at the heart of Pictish territory – the Picts trounced a Viking army here in AD 903 – and there are many standing stones around.

BRUACH NA FRITHE (3,143 feet)
Get a good up-to-date guide and pick a walker's way up this Munro on Skye. I recommend going up Fionn Choire. This way you can do a wee detour to Sgurr a Bhasteir and admire the antics of the climbers on the Bhasteir tooth – but watch the weather and mind that coming down can be much harder (one fine spring day I ended up sliding 20 feet on my bum). The view at the top is spectacular. From the summit you can see much of the main ridge, while you open your Thermos and listen to the fibs of other ridge walkers. There is a fine description of ascending the peak in *The Last Enemy* (1942) by fighter pilot Richard Hillary.

BUACHAILLE ETIVE MOR (3,352 feet)
This is the mountain (Buachaille pronounced 'buckle') that seems to guard the entrance to Glencoe from the south. It

stands at the head of beautiful Glen Etive (the name means 'Big Shepherd of Etive'), and can be ascended from the flank by Coire na Tulaich.

EILDON HILL (1,385 feet)
A rather gentler walk than some of the other hills here, this was a hill fort (the ramparts survive) 1,000 years before the Romans arrived and built their fort Trimontium (named after Eildon's three peaks) at the foot of the hill by the Tweed. This is a fairy hill, and is where Thomas the Rhymer met the Queen of Elfland.

SUILVEN (2,389 feet)
A dramatically isolated mountain in the north-west, Suilven's name derives from old Norse, and means 'Pillar Mountain'. The mountain is less difficult to climb than it looks, but the final gully is a slog. Suilven derives its prominence from being an 'inselberg' or 'island mountain': a sandstone remnant perching on a bed of ancient Lewisian gneiss.

—— Six Great Rivers ——

CLYDE (106 miles long)
'Glasgow made the Clyde, and the Clyde made Glasgow' is the old summary of the relationship between the city and its river, which was dredged for both shipbuilding and trade. *The Queen Elizabeth*, *Queen Mary* and *QE2* were Clyde-built, and ships continue to be built here. The Clyde used to be heavily polluted, but now supports a healthy population of fish.

DEE (80 miles long)
Renowned for its spring run of salmon, the Dee rises in the Cairngorms and flows through the Grampians, entering the

North Sea at Aberdeen. The area around Braemar and Ballater is known as 'Royal Deeside': Victoria spent the summers here at Balmoral Castle and the area has been popular with royals (and tourists) ever since.

FORTH *(65 miles long)*
The Forth is the main river of the Central Belt plain, and has been vitally important to the industrial development of Scotland: it runs from the Trossachs, on through Stirling, and then into the Firth of Forth. Its meandering course across the history-soaked plain is best viewed from the Wallace Monument.

SPEY *(107 miles long)*
The Spey is the second longest river in Scotland, and the fastest. It runs through the tourist heartland of the Central Highlands, from Newtonmore and Kingussie to Aviemore, ending at the Moray Firth. A great salmon river, its banks are also the setting for some of Scotland's great whisky distilleries.

TAY *(120 miles long)*
The Tay is the longest Scottish river, and is also the largest British river in volume. A prime salmon river, it flows through Perth, and Dundee sits on the northern bank of its firth.

TWEED *(97 miles long)*
The Tweed rises at Tweedsmuir, close to where the Clyde also rises, and flows through Peebles and Kelso before reaching the North Sea at Berwick-upon-Tweed. For much of its distance it marks the border between Scotland and England. Like the Spey and Tay, the Tweed is one of Scotland's great fishing rivers, indeed is regarded by many as the greatest salmon-fishing river in the world. One of its tributaries is the slow-moving Till, a relationship marked by this chilling old rhyme:

Scotland—10

Says Tweed tae Till
'Whit gars ye rin sae still?'
Says Till tae Tweed
'Though ye rin wi' speed
And I rin slaw,
For ae man that ye droon
I droon twa.'

—— The First Peoples of Scotland ——

The first settlers in Scotland seem to have been hunter-gatherers who arrived here after the retreat of the glaciers, about 10,000 years ago (the Mesolithic Age), but we know very little of these people: Scottish prehistory really takes off in the Neolithic or 'New' Stone Age, about 4,000 years ago, with the arrival of farmers from Europe. These settlers may or may not have merged with the first inhabitants – or killed, or driven them off, and changed the look of Scotland dramatically by deforestation (at least that is the current wisdom – previously the Vikings or Tudor shipbuilders got the blame).

—— Six Great Prehistoric Sites ——
(and a recent stone circle)

CALLANISH

Callanish is on the island of Lewis. The Lewisian gneiss rocks found in the Outer Hebrides and north-west of Scotland are the oldest rocks in Europe, and were used by Neolithic people to create one of the most impressive prehistoric stone circles in Europe. Martin Martin wrote in his *A Description of the Western Islands of Scotland c. 1695* (1703): 'I enquired of the inhabitants what tradition they had from their ancestors concerning these stones; and they told me, it was a place appointed for worship in the time of heathenism, and that the chief druid or priest stood near the big stone in the centre, from whence he addressed himself to the people that surrounded him.'

Dating from around 2000 BC, Callanish was built long before there were any records of Druids, and seems to be earlier than Stonehenge.

KILMARTIN
Kilmartin Glen in Argyll is one of the least known prehistoric sites in Europe, and one of the most remarkable. There are over 350 ancient monuments in mid-Argyll, 150 of them pre-historic. The glen has 'standing stones, burial cairns, rock art, forts, duns and carved stones', and is a veritable theme park for the archaeologist: a haunting landscape whose monuments stretch back millennia, and include Christian monuments dating from the sixth century. The fort of Dunadd here is thought to have been the capital of the ancient kingdom of Dalriada; its 'royal inauguration' stone footprint in which generations of Scottish kings may have placed their feet is actually a replica (but feels real enough).

MAESHOWE
The ancient settlement of Maeshowe on Orkney was uncovered in 1861. It dates from around 2700 BC and is one of the finest chambered cairns anywhere. (Orcadians in the 1860s didn't think much of the mound, regarding it as the home of a dreadful creature with a dreadful name, the hugboy.) Maeshowe was broken into at some point by Vikings, who left some intriguing runic graffiti, for example: 'Haermund Hardaxe carved these runes' and 'Ingigerth is the most beautiful of all women'.

Mousa Broch

The broch is one of the few forms of architecture original to Scotland. A broch is a tall tower built using dry stones, with concentric walls which incorporate stairs and living accommodation: the area at the bottom would have housed animals. Brochs could have been used for local gatherings, or for defensive purposes. They were solidly built and most would probably still be standing were it not for people through the ages carting off the stones.

Most brochs are little more than ruins, and the most impressive survivor is the broch on the wee Shetland island of Mousa which has stood for around 2,000 years and is now home to a cacophonous colony of storm petrels.

Ring of Brodgar

Built on Orkney between 3000 and 2000 BC, the Ring of Brodgar would be an impressive stone circle anywhere, but its situation on its thin strip of land – between salt and fresh water – is highly dramatic. Along with Maeshowe, the Stenness standing stones and other ancient monuments, Brodgar is part of a UNESCO World Heritage Site.

Skara Brae

Orkney's Skara Brae is Europe's most complete Neolithic village. The group of ten houses (complete with stone shelves) was inhabited between 3,200 and 2,200 years ago, and discovered in 1850. It is a UNESCO World Heritage Site.

Sighthill Stone Circle

The Sighthill Stone Circle was in Sighthill Park, Glasgow, overlooking the M8 motorway. Constructed in (AD!) 1978–9 as part of the Glasgow Parks Astronomy Project (and completed at the spring equinox), it was the first astronomically aligned circle built in Britain for several thousand years. It looked very authentic – and should in theory have been a great city attraction. Alas, the site of the circle was both lonely and exposed, and an unsupervised visit was definitely not recommended. In 2016, the circle was removed by the council, to be relocated elsewhere.

—— The Romans in Scotland ——

Recorded Scottish history begins with the arrival of the Romans. The emperor Claudius invaded Britain in AD 43 and over the next few decades the legions moved north fighting some tribes and making accommodations with others, moving the frontier of the empire onwards. The Romans referred to the people in Scotland as 'Caledonians' and our image of these people is derived from Tacitus, who describes large-limbed, red-haired men, somewhat like a 1950s Aberdeen centre-half. The Romans recognized these tribes as distinct from the Britons in south-west Scotland (who spoke a form of early Welsh, and whose capital was at Dumbarton).

A series of forts was established at the limit of Roman expansion about AD 70 along the Gask Ridge in Perthshire. The Gask Ridge system is the earliest known fortified Roman frontier anywhere in the empire. Around AD 83, the Romans had a resounding victory over the Caledonians at Mons Graupius. By AD 100, however, the Romans had over-extended themselves and withdrew to a line along the Tyne–Solway isthmus.

HADRIAN'S WALL
Shortly after the retreat from the Gask Ridge, the Romans began building a chain of forts from the Solway to the Tyne

along a road subsequently dubbed the Stanegate. The wall was constructed after the emperor Hadrian's visit in AD 122 and was probably complete by AD 132. Much of the wall – now a UNESCO World Heritage Site – remains more or less intact, if not as high or as broad as it was: at its largest, the wall was 20 feet high and 20 feet wide; sections up to 10 feet high survive. The wall is one of the most important remaining fixtures of the Roman Empire; over 73 miles long, it runs from Wallesend-on-Tyne in the east to Bowness-on-Solway in the west. It is made of stone and turf and was dotted with forts along the way. The wall is now of course entirely in England, but don't let that put you off. There are few places in the world where you can feel the Scottish past so present as on a walk along this wall. Soldiers from all over the empire were stationed here, and funeral monuments testify to the multiracial nature of the wall and its inhabitants: a Syrian merchant called Barates trading at the fort called Arbeia ('Place of the Arabs') left a memorial to his wife Regina, a former slave who was a member of the Cattivellauni tribe in what is now Kent.

VINDOLANDA

The first fort at Vindolanda was built around AD 80, and occupied a central position on the Stanegate supply route. It was built of timber: such forts were usually rebuilt about every eight years, and by the time Hadrian's Wall was built, Vindolanda would likely have been on to its sixth incarnation. The successive layers had clay and turf laid over them by the army builders, and this created anaerobic conditions which have preserved many remains of great significance, most notably private letters written on thin wood tablets which give wonderful insights into Roman life on the wall. One of the tablets is the oldest surviving letter from one woman to another, a charming birthday invitation. It begins: 'Claudia Severa to her Lepidina greetings. On 11 September, sister, for the day of the celebration of my birthday, I give you a warm invitation…'

Vindolanda was still occupied in the sixth century, long after the death of the empire.

ANTONINE WALL

The Antonine Wall is the last of the three fortified frontiers built here by the Romans and is the most northerly point of the Roman Empire. The wall stretches for 367 miles from Bo'ness on the Forth to Old Kilpatrick on the Clyde. Construction began around AD 142 during the reign of the emperor Antoninus Pius. The wall is a turf rampart on a stone foundation, and was a much more basic affair than Hadrian's Wall. Its purpose was to extend the range of the empire, but eventually the troops fell back to Hadrian's Wall. Rough Castle, near Falkirk, is the best preserved of the wall forts. In 1996 a magnificent stone sculpture of a lioness devouring a man was found in the River Almond, by the strategically important garrison of Cramond. The Antonine Wall was abandoned around AD 160.

—— The Emergence of the Picts ——

The word 'Picti' is a Roman term meaning 'painted' or 'tattooed' people. It is not recorded until shortly before Constantine was proclaimed emperor in York in AD 306. It is possible that 'Picti' originated as a handy Roman name for a confederation of tribes who included (or were descended from) the Caledonians.

—— The Scottish Peoples After the Romans ——

A great many people came to Scotland after the Romans. The Scots came in from Ireland; Norwegians and other Scandinavians came in waves after the early eighth century; the Irish came into the Central Belt in large numbers in the nineteenth and early twentieth centuries; and in the twentieth century Italians, South Asians and others joined us, as did (after 2004) large numbers of Poles.

On the debit side, in the early seventeenth century large numbers of Lowland Scots settled in Ulster (or in the long view, returned to Ulster), and the eighteenth and nineteenth centuries saw thousands of Highlanders leave, many of them unwillingly. See The Scots Abroad: Emigration and the Clearances, p. 245.

—— Scottish Regions ——

The different regions of Scotland are as follows, starting at the top with Orkney and Shetland.

ORKNEY AND SHETLAND

Maps of Scotland often show Orkney and Shetland in a box at the top right-hand side, a few millimetres away from John O'Groats. In fact, the capital of Shetland, Lerwick, is much closer to Bergen in Norway than it is to Edinburgh, and both Orcadians and Shetlanders have tended to regard themselves as being at least as much Norwegian as Scottish, and speak of travelling to Scotland when they go south.

Shetland has over 100 islands, of which around 16 are inhabited. Mainland is the biggest. Orkney has about 70 islands (some are big rocks, really), of which some 30 are inhabited.

Both Orkney and Shetland were colonized by Vikings in the late eighth century. The question of what happened to the original inhabitants, whether wiped out or absorbed, remains debated. Both Orkney and Shetland were annexed by Harold Harfagre ('Fair Hair') for Norway in AD 875. The islands and their people became forfeit to Scotland in 1468–9 in lieu of an unpaid Norse dowry.

THE HEBRIDES

The Hebrides comprise the Outer Hebrides – the islands of Barra, Harris, Lewis, the Uists (North and South, and the smaller isles of Berneray, Benbecula and Eriskay) and St Kilda – and the Inner Hebrides, Islay, Jura, Skye, Mull, Raasay, Staffa and the Small Isles (principally Canna, Rum, Eigg and Muck).

Most of Scotland's Gaelic speakers come from the Outer or Western Isles, which came under Norwegian rule in the ninth century, following widespread Viking settlement, and became part of Scotland with the Treaty of Perth in 1266. It took many centuries, however, for the Scottish kings to stamp their authority on the Western Isles. In 1598, James VI gave the splendidly named 'Gentleman Adventurers of Fife' land on Lewis to colonize, following the forfeiture to the king of those MacLeod lands. Predictably it all ended badly, and the colonial expedition failed amid the customary violence and treachery (see p. 109).

THE HIGHLANDS

The traditional definition of the Scottish Highlands is that part of northern Scotland that lies to the north-west of the Highland Boundary Fault, from Dumbarton in the west to Stonehaven in the east; thus Aberdeen and its environs are not Highland, but Inverness is. The term is normally inclusive of the Hebrides, but not Orkney and Shetland.

The Highlands, even if one includes the scattered townships, still form one of the most sparsely populated areas in Europe. Yet it was not always so: as has often been pointed out, the romantic-seeming glens of the Highlands are places haunted by their past populations; this region saw a huge reduction in the number of its inhabitants in the eighteenth and nineteenth centuries.

The area was almost entirely Gaelic-speaking until the early nineteenth century, and clan-based. Clans have come and gone, with the MacDonalds, MacLeods, Frasers, Campbells, Stewarts, Mackays, Macleans and Camerons being among the great survivors.

The Central Belt
The term 'Scottish Lowlands' is usually taken to include all that area south and east of the Highlands. The Central Belt is that part of the Lowlands lying between the Highlands and the Southern Uplands on the English border. This is the most heavily populated part of Scotland and was the heartland of the Industrial Revolution, from the shipyards of the Clyde to the jute mills of Dundee. The people of the Central Belt are a mixture of Scots, Irish, English and now also many others, including South Asian and Polish. In 1750 this part of Scotland was agricultural, yet only fifty years later it was industrialized, and is now largely post-industrial.

The Borders
The Scottish border with England now conjures up rugby, textiles and tourism, with wee teashops serving scones with

cream and jam. But up until the mid-seventeenth century this was one of the most dangerous regions of Europe. Beguiling and beautiful as the Borders can be, the Borderers are the people who gave us such terms as blackmail and red-handed. Even the place names evoke danger: Foulbogskye, Hungry Hill, Wolf Rig, Foulplay Know, Flodden, Blackhaggs, the Debatable Land; as George MacDonald Fraser says in his masterly history of the Border reivers, *The Steel Bonnets* (1971), this is 'obviously not a palm-fringed playground'. Even the family 'riding' surnames sound warlike: Kerr, Kang, Armstrong. Some of the toughest of the Border families were not all that determinedly Scottish; in truth, cross-border outfits such as the Armstrongs and the Grahams had family and friends in the English Marches, and many enemies on their 'own' side.

—— Six Scottish Cities ——

Here are wee snapshots of the six major Scottish cities.

ABERDEEN *(population c.200,000)*
Dubbed 'the Granite City' (or 'Silver City'), Aberdeen has a remarkable skyline and can be quite startlingly beautiful after the rain, when the city actually sparkles thanks to the mica in the stone (rain is not uncommon here). Plants love the climate, and there are many fine parks and gardens, and a long beach. The council likes the city to be known as 'Oil Capital of Europe' as Aberdeen is close to the North Sea oil reserves.

DUNDEE *(population c.145,000)*
In the declining days of the empire, Dundee was known to generations of schoolchildren as the city of jam, jute and journalism, a great trading city at the mouth of the Tay. The jam

was actually Keiller's marmalade, and the jute was imported from South Asia and processed in the city's mills, the last of which closed in the mid-1960s. The journalism was the work of the extraordinary firm of DC Thomson & Co, which still produces over 200 million magazines a year, and comics such as the *Dandy* and *Beano*. Its newspapers include the *Sunday Post* (motto: 'A thoroughly decent read') which has a circulation of over 400,000 in Scotland. In the late 1980s Dundee rebranded itself as 'the City of Discovery', a marketing slogan which is actually a fair reflection of the city's great sailing and whaling past.

EDINBURGH *(population c.460,000)*

One of the world's most beautiful cities: there is much to do and see and most of it is within walking distance, from Dean Village to the Royal Mile. Lovely as Edinburgh is, it has social problems. Optimists will tell you that things have moved on since Irvine Welsh's novel *Trainspotting*; pessimists will say yes, it's got worse. (*The Everyman Edinburgh Guide* (2008) was written by the present author.)

GLASGOW *(population c.580,000, but over a million if you count the satellite areas)*

Scotland's biggest city, Glasgow's name means 'Dear Green Place' in Gaelic, and despite becoming one of the great industrial and shipbuilding cities, the nineteenth-century planners ensured that the city had fine parks open to all. Glasgow remains essentially a nineteenth-century city, and (despite the resolute efforts of city planners) retains many of its fine buildings. It also, alas, retains much poverty and inadequate social housing, and parts of the city have the lowest life expectancy in Europe.

INVERNESS *(population c.70,000)*

Inverness calls itself the capital of the Highlands, and is situated at the mouth of the River Ness. The town site has been settled since the early sixth century, when it was a Pictish stronghold. After Poland joined the EU in 2004, Inverness quickly became a favourite destination for Polish workers, and the Polish population of the city has been estimated in 2008 at 10 per cent of the total, which would mean that there are twice as many Polish speakers in Inverness as there are Gaelic speakers.

STIRLING *(population c.40,000)*

An ancient settlement with a fine strategic position on the Forth, and sited on a crag at the foot of the Ochil Hills, Stirling was granted royal burgh status in 1130, and became a city in 2002. The old fort has seen many invaders since at least Roman times to the arrival of the Jacobite army in 1746, and it has been reasonably suggested that the name 'Stirling' means 'place of strife'.

—— Royal Burghs ——

Royal burghs were Scottish towns or cities that had been awarded a royal charter confirming the burgh's rights to regulate the lives of its population, and to appoint bailies (magistrates) with often wide-ranging powers. Most royal burghs were seaports such as St Andrews and Rothesay, and there were seventy of them by 1707 (an easy figure to remember). The status of royal burgh was abolished in 1975 and most such towns now call themselves 'former royal burghs'.

2

The Scots Languages

❖

Scotland has three main recognized languages: Scottish English (the form of English in modern everyday usage in Scotland), Scots or Lallans (the old form of English spoken in Scotland, now mainly found in rural Lowland areas) and Gaelic. In practice, an English speaker from an old mining town in Lanarkshire and an English speaker from rural Aberdeenshire may struggle to communicate effectively without some compromising drop into 'standard' English, and a Lallans speaker may find they have as many words in common with an Ulster person who speaks Ullans, the Northern Irish form of Lallans, as with a fellow Scot speaking the Glasgow version of Scottish English.

—— Old Scots ——

What is not in doubt is that old Scots was a wonderfully expressive language. Here are some examples of what a powerful, direct, yet often poetic means of communication the Scots language could be.

Gavin Dunbar, Archbishop of Glasgow

In 1524, infuriated by the depredations of the Border reivers, Glasgow's archbishop let fly with one of the greatest ecclesiastical curses of all time, which was read throughout the diocese. Here is a small extract:

I curse their heid and all the haris of thair heid; I curse thair face, thair ene, thair mouth, thair neise, thair tongue, thair teeth, thair crag, thair shoulderis, thair breist, thair hert, thair stomok, thair bak, thair wame, thair armes, thais leggis, thair handis, thair feit, and everilk part of thair body, frae the top of their heid to the soill of thair feet, befoir and behind, within and without.

I curse thaim gangand, and I curse them rydand; I curse thaim standand, and I curse thaim sittand; I curse thaim etand, I curse thaim drinkand; I curse thaim walkand, I curse thaim sleepand; I curse thaim risand, I curse thaim lyand; I curse thaim at hame, I curse thaim fra hame; I curse thaim within the house, I curse thaim without the house; I curse thair wiffis, thair barnis, and thair servandis participand with thaim in their deides. I wary thair cornys, thair catales, thair woll, thair scheip, thjair horse, thair swyne, thair geise, thair hennes, and all thair quyk gude. I wary their hallis, thair chalmeris, thair kechingis, thair stanillis, thair barnys, thair biris, thair bernyardis, thair cailyardis, thair plewis, thair harrowis, and the gudis and housis that is necessair for their sustentatioun and weilfair.

JAMES BOSWELL
(Imagining how he would tell Rousseau in Scots that he need not be such an oddball):

Hoot, Johnie Rousseau mon, what for hae ye sae mony figmangairies? You're a bonny man indeed to mauk siccan a wark; set ye up. Canna ye just live like ither fowk?

LORD BRAXFIELD, SCOTLAND'S 'HANGING JUDGE'
(On being told that Jesus was a reformer):

Muckle he made o' that. He was hanget.

(Whispering to a juror at a trial of political radicals):

Come awa, Maister Horner, come awa, and help us to hang ane o' thae damned scoondrels.

LORD KAMES

(Saying goodbye to his fellow judges in 1782):

Fare ye a' weel, ye bitches!

SIR WALTER SCOTT

'And what would you have me to do,' answered the fisher gruffly, 'unless I wanted to see four children starve, because ane is drowned? It's weel wi' you gentles, that can sit in the house wi' handkerchers at your een when ye lose a friend; but the like o' us maun to our wark again, if our hearts were beating as hard as my hammer.' (*The Antiquary*, chapter 34)

'Troth, I was e'en thinking sae,' replied Andrew, dogmatically; 'for if your honour disna ken when ye hae a gude servant, I ken when I hae a gude master, and the deil be in my feet gin I leave ye – and there's the brief and the lang o't besides I hae received nae regular warning to quit my place.' (*Rob Roy*, chapter 24)

'How fell that, sir? Speak out, sir, and do not Maister or Campbell me – my foot is on my native heath, and my name is MacGregor!' (*Rob Roy*, chapter 34)

'Why,' resumed MacGregor, 'ye ken weel eneugh that women and gear are at the bottom of a' the mischief in this warld.' (*Rob Roy*, chapter 35)

'I dinna ken muckle about the law,' answered Mrs. Howden; 'but I ken, when we had a king, and a chancellor, and parliament men o' our ain, we could aye peeble them wi' stanes when they werena gude bairns – But naebody's nails can reach the length o' Lunnon.' (*The Heart of Midlothian*, chapter 4)

ROBERT LOUIS STEVENSON

There was nae doubt, onyway, but that Mr. Soulis had been ower lang at the college… He had a feck o' books wi' him – mair than had ever been seen before in a' that presbytery; and a sair wark the carrier had wi' them, for they were a' like to have smoored in the Deil's Hag between this and Kilmackerlie. They were books o' divinity, to be sure, or so they ca'd them; but the serious were o' opinion there was little service for sae mony, when the hail o' God's Word would gang in the neuk of a plaid. ('Thrawn Janet')

—— Scottish English ——

As indicated above, discussion of Scottish English can get rather heated. The coward's way out of what can be a linguistic minefield would be to say go to YouTube and call up everything under 'Teach Scottish' where you will find many – often highly funny – examples of English as it is currently spoken in (mostly urban) Scotland.

ACCENTS BY REGION
Glasgow (and much of the West Central Belt): Glasgow has a rich local dialect, documented in *The Patter* (1996) by Scots author Mike Munro. This selection of facial similes is taken

(with permission) from the 2006 edition. A face like:

> a bulldog chowin a wasp
> a burst couch
> a camel eatin sherbet
> a Hallowe'en cake
> a melted welly
> a ruptured hot-water bottle
> a wee hard disease
> a well-skelped arse
> somebody sat on it before it was set
> ye never sugared his tea

Doric: Doric, the language spoken in Aberdeen and the rest of the north-east, is actually a version of Lallans rather than Scottish English. Either way, Aberdonian speech is often incomprehensible to Lowland Scots, especially Glaswegians, who picture Aberdonians going about saying charming things such as, 'Fit like, keelie?' i.e. 'How are you, urban thug?'

Many Doric terms sound implausible but are usually genuine, such as the following:

foggy bummer	bumblebee
loun	young lad
quine (or quean)	young woman

Some Doric expressions:

a man mon hae mait	a man must eat
a poultice for a timmer	i.e. something useless
[wooden] **leg**	
gang yer ain gait	go your own way

Orkney: For around 1,000 years – from c.850 to the eighteenth century – the language of Orkney was 'norn', a variant of old Norse. There are norn survivals in the Orkney dialect, but many Orcadians would agree that there has been a huge decline in the use and understanding of the islanders' speech.

Here are some examples of Orkney words:

gavse	eat ravenously
gelder	laugh
moppy	rabbit
nareaboots	nearly
peedie	small
puggy	belly
skreck	shriek
skreevar	strong wind
waar	worse
whitema	seagull

Shetland: Norn died out in Shetland, as in Orkney, but rather later – in the late nineteenth century. Shetlandic is distinct from Orcadian and has been famously described as a form of English taught by Lowland Scots to Norwegians. Shetlandic is basically Scottish English grafted on to a Norse base.

Shetlandic is in a healthier state than Orcadian, and there are many thriving websites devoted to the language.

baess maet	cattle food
blinkie	torch
buggle-day	feast day
flankers	tall rubber boots
maddertim	temper tantrum
makkin	knitting
paese be wi dee	peace be with you
shuggy	drizzly

| **wadder** | weather |
| **yarta** | darlin |

For an invaluable guide to Scotland's regional accents, visit
www.scotslanguage.com, where you can click on a map of the
regions and hear what the locals sound like and if you click
on the red button you can browse the site in either English or
Scots. Brilliant: this is what the web is for.

GAELIC

It used to be said that the clearest English speakers in the world
came from Inverness, a consequence (allegedly) of native
Gaelic speakers bypassing Scottish English and Lallans and
learning 'pure' English. There are probably a host of unlovely
assumptions hidden within that belief, but certainly Gaelic
speakers are renowned for their diction.

Gaelic has enjoyed a renaissance in Scotland, and is being
taught and learned outside its 'Gaidhealtachd' heartland. Here
are some handy phrases:

> **Madainn mhath (**mateen[1] vah)
> Good morning
>
> **Feasgar math** (face gar mah)
> Good afternoon or evening
>
> **Oidhche mhath** (oy chi[2] vah)
> Good night
>
> **Ciamar a tha sibh?** (kamar a ha shiv)
> How are you?

---

[1] The softer sound of a Gaelic 't', and usually 'd' is formed by
placing the tongue against the back of the top front teeth. Not
unlike Spanish '*tapas*'.

[2] **ch** as in loch, **i** as in bit.

To which the usual response is:
Tha gu math (ha goo mah)
Fine

followed by:
Ciamar a tha sibh fhein? (kamar a ha shiv hain)
How are you yourself?

Tapadh leibh (tah pa leev or live[3])
Thank you (formal, or to more than one person)

Tapadh leat (tah pa laht)
Thank you (to someone you know well)

Mòran taing (more an tang)
Many thanks

Slàinte mhath (slaan tchi[4] vah)
Your good health

Slàinte mhòr (vore)
Your great health – reputedly a secret toast to Bonnie Prince Charlie, Mòr also being a Gaelic variant for Marion/Mary, i.e. a woman, Charlie having been disguised as a serving maid

Chaidh an ceòl air feadh na fìdhle (cha-ee an kyawl air fey-ugh[5] na fee-li)
There was uproar (lit. the fiddle went throughout the music)

---

3   rhyme with five (pronunciation of many words, including **leibh**, varies from place to place. In general, follow the accent of the person you are talking to where possible).

4   **tch** as in church, **i** as in bit

5   **gh**: this sound is made by sounding, or voicing, **ch** as in loch

Tha mo cheann na bhrochan (ha mo chyown[6] na vrochan)
My brain's in a pickle (lit. my head is full of porridge)

Cho sgìth ris a' chù (cho[7] skee reesh a choo)
as tired as the dog, e.g.
Tha mi (ha mee) **cho sgìth ris a' chù**
I'm dog tired

Beannachd leibh (bjan[8]-achk live)
A blessing go with you (formal, or to more than one person)

Beannachd leat (bjan-achk laht)
A blessing go with you (to someone you know well)

Tìoraidh (cheery)
cheerio

—— Slogans ——

A slogan is a Highland clan battle cry – from the Gaelic 'sluagh-ghairm' (sloo-agh ghar-am) for 'host-cry' – but Lowland clans also had them (and needed them in mêlées). Some notable ones are:

Bruce   **Fuimus:** We were once
             (a curiously poignant war cry)

Campbell   **Cruachan** (kroo-achan, ch as in
             loch): i.e. Ben Cruachan

---

6   rhyme with crown
7   **cho** rhymes with so
8   **bj** as in Swedish Bjorn

Donald	**Per Mare per Terras**: By sea by land
Gregor	**S Rioghal Mo Dhream** (sree-ghal mo ghraim): Royal is my race
Johnstone	**Light Thieves All** (a demand to surrender)
MacArthur	**Eisd, O Eisd** (ays-tch, as in church): Listen, O Listen
Mackinnon	**Cuimhnich bas Alpein** (Kuy-nyich baas alpeen, ch as in loch): Remember the death of Alpin
Mackintosh	**Loch Moy**
Macleod	**Hold Fast**
Scott	**A Bellendain** (Bellendain was at the heart of Scott territory)
Seton	**Seton! And set on!**

Many Scottish towns (especially in the Borders) also had their slogans:

Dumfries	**A Loreburn!** A Loreburn!
Duns	**Duns Dings A'**
Falkirk	**Better meddle wi the deil as the bairns o' Falkirk** (Falkirk FC are called the 'Bairns' after this slogan)
Forfar	**Farfar will be Farfar still**
Jedburgh	**Jethart's Here!**
Kelso	**Dae Richt, Fear Nocht**

3

FAUNA AND FLORA

❖

—— Fauna ——

Most of the wildlife in Scotland moved in at the same time as humans, when the glaciers retreated around 10,000 years ago. And long before then, there were the dinosaurs.

SCOTTISH DINOSAURS

Dinosaur fossils are not common in Scotland, but recently several remarkable finds have been made on Skye, demonstrating that Scotland's ancient geographical links are with North America rather than Europe, with coelophysis bones being discovered which perfectly match ones found in New Mexico. Several bones of both theropods and sauropods, and even a 'trackway' of theropod footprints (made by a group of carnosaurs, possibly megalosaurs) have been discovered on Skye. The island now holds several dinosaur records: the oldest coelophysid, the world's first evidence of a theropod family group (the footprints of an adult ornithopod found with the footprints of young of the same species), the earliest anklyosaur-type dinosaur, and the smallest dinosaur footprint ever found. The Staffin Museum on Skye has an excellent display of local dinosaur fossils and will advise on field trips.

Skye is proving to be a happy hunting ground for seekers of dinosaur fossils. In 2015, a remarkable series of sauropod footprints was discovered near Duntulm; the largest dinosaur site yet found in Britain. The quantity of footprints has led to the site being dubbed the 'dinosaur disco'. The trackways date from *c*.170 million years ago and provide evidence for the first time that sauropods spent time in coastal areas, and waded in shallow water.

EXTINCT MAMMALS

In the time of the Romans, Caledonia was famous for its **bears**, and the poet Martial describes a Caledonian bear being offered a prisoner hanging on a cross in the Colosseum in Rome. How long bears survived in Scotland is debated: they may possibly have survived until the eighth or ninth centuries. Our ancestors probably hunted **beaver** out by the fourteenth century. It used to be thought that the **lynx** became extinct in Britain about 4,000 years ago but recent bone discoveries have brought the lynx into early medieval times. The **wild boar** (a popular figure on Pictish monuments) probably became extinct in Scotland in the thirteenth century. Popular tradition claims that the last **wolf** in Britain was near the Findhorn River in 1743. In fact, all we can be reasonably sure about is that there were still wolves in Scotland *c*.1600 and we can be pretty certain that they were wiped out by the late seventeenth century. **Beaver** have now been released in Argyll and have successfully bred; the reintroduction has not been universally welcome, however, and at least twenty beavers (some pregnant) have been shot.The possibility of wolves and bears being reintroduced is remote.

EXTANT MAMMALS

There are eight species of **bats** in Scotland with others (non-derogatively known as 'vagrant' species) dropping in from time to time. All British bat species are protected. One pipistrelle can consume 3,000 insects (including the fearsome midges) in an evening. Scotland's two species of **deer** are red and roe.

There are around 300,000 red deer in Scotland, mostly in the Highlands. Roe deer are much smaller, tend to be loners, and favour woodland. The Scottish **mountain hare** is very similar to the Irish mountain hare, but the Scottish one turns white in the winter. It has a pleasing Latin name: *Lepus timidus scoticus*. Scotland's **otter** population is one of the healthiest in Europe, and they can be found all year long throughout Scotland, in rivers, lochs and along the coast. Ignore advice (often given) to find otters by looking for droppings (called 'spraint' – leave that pastime to otter-shit experts). Watch the water, and, if by the sea, watch the beach as well as the water. Otters play a lot and often make themselves visible. The **pine marten** is a rare creature based in heavily wooded Highland areas. It is the only mustelid with semi-retractable claws, enabling it to scramble up and down trees with ease. The **red fox** has in recent years become an urban animal, eating leftover kebabs and fish suppers. Like its ancient foe the pine marten, the **red squirrel** is an endangered animal that is now making a comeback.

Scotland's **wild goats** are descended from escaped domestic goats and now abound all over Scotland, particularly in upland and coastal areas. The Scottish **wildcat** is a unique and separate species of cat: formerly regarded as vermin, the main threat to the species now comes from interbreeding with both feral and domestic cats.

CETACEANS AND SEALS

The **bottlenose dolphin** is commonly seen around Scotland's coasts, with the population in the Moray Firth being the best known. The Moray Firth colony shares its territory with the smaller **harbour porpoise**, which is Scotland's most abundant cetacean. In recent years, it has been discovered that Moray Firth dolphins have attacked and killed their smaller cousins (one attack has been filmed), a discovery that led to such behaviour being identified elsewhere in the world. The first recorded case of 'infanticide' among cetaceans was also observed among the Moray Firth dolphin colony. **Killer whales** are the biggest dolphins, and can grow to 25 feet and weigh 6 tons. This species, the apex predator in the ocean, can be seen all around Scotland in spring and summer. They are unmistakable in appearance, with a huge dorsal fin, and travel in groups called pods. They hunt fish and seals and other cetaceans. The most common whale in Scottish waters (from April to October) is the **minke**, though humpbacks are also occasionally seen. Scotland has two species of **seal**: grey and common. Grey seals are larger, prefer the rockier west coast of Scotland, and make up around 40 per cent of the world population. Scottish common seals make up around 90 per cent of the UK seal population.

A REPTILE AND AN INSECT

The **adder** is the only poisonous snake in Britain, and is the only British snake with a zigzag pattern on its back. Adders can be spotted when basking on rocks on warm summer days, and are therefore not often noticed. The **midge** causes more misery to humans than any other species of animal in Scotland. Midges are tiny swarming insects which like damp, temperate conditions, and only the females bite. The accepted wisdom is that the further north and west you go, the worse they get. Skye midges are particularly feared, and can even be found plaguing scramblers on the Cuillin Ridge. They do, however, provide lots of food for bats and birds. Be prepared, very prepared.

FISH

At 30 feet long and weighing 7 tons the **basking shark** is the second biggest fish in the world, and a summer visitor to Scotland in increasing numbers. This magnificent fish is completely harmless to humans, being a plankton eater. The **Atlantic salmon** is one of Scotland's iconic animals, and a valuable food resource that has been protected under Scots law since at least the fourteenth century. Scotland is regarded as having some of the finest salmon rivers in the world, but the species has undergone a steep decline. Many Scottish waters have been stocked with **rainbow trout**, but it is the native **brown trout** – the 'brownie' – that retains the affection of locals and tourists. Scottish trout come in all shapes and sizes, from wee burn to the huge 'ferox' trout in the large lochs such as Loch Awe. **Pike** can be found in any big river or canal in Scotland, but it is the lochs that provide a steady supply of large specimens: the British record, over 47 pounds, was taken in Loch Lomond.

Birds

The **capercaillie** is a large woodland grouse and lives in pine woods and conifer plantations. An endangered species, you may see them in the wild at the Loch Garten Reserve.The **raven** is the largest crow. Folk myths about this highly intelligent animal abound throughout the world, and the bird is a common presence in Scottish story and song. Three species of **crossbill** (a finch species) inhabit the Caledonian Forest: the common crossbill, the parrot crossbill, and the Scottish crossbill. The last was identified as a separate species in 1980, but the identification remains controversial: ornithologists disagree over whether or not it is indeed a separate species. If so, it is the only endemic bird species in the British Isles. The iconic Scottish **golden eagle** is a magnificent creature soaring above the hills and high ground. (If you see an eagle sitting on a fence post, it will be a buzzard – an equally splendid bird.) Eagles were formerly persecuted throughout the Highlands and are still being poisoned, their bodies usually being found near 'sporting' estates. The **red grouse** is an upland game bird, most often encountered by walkers through heather moorland as it rises out of cover when approached. The **hoodie crow** is an intelligent creature with dark habits (suspected of pecking out the eyes of newborn lambs), and thus features in many Scottish songs and tales. 'The Tale of the Hoodie' is one of the best known Scottish folk tales. The **ptarmigan** is a partridge-like game bird that breeds on the mountains. If you see a plump bird scurrying away from you while hillwalking, it is likely to be a ptarmigan.

REINTRODUCTIONS AND NEW ARRIVALS

Several species of bird became extinct in historical times in Scotland and have been successfully reintroduced, the most dramatic example being the **white-tailed eagle** (or **sea eagle**) which was once, and is now again, the biggest British bird, and fourth largest eagle anywhere. It was hunted to extinction in the early 1900s, and there are now around forty breeding pairs in the west of Scotland. The **osprey** was wiped out in Scotland by egg collectors in the late nineteenth century. A pair returned to breed at Loch Garten in 1959 (still the best place to see them) and one female has raised chicks here since 1991. The **red kite** became extinct in Scotland round about 1870 and was reintroduced in 1990. There are now some eighty breeding pairs, but, as with golden eagles and other birds of prey, it is not uncommon for poisoned specimens to be found, often near sporting estates.

The formidable predator **eagle owl** became extinct here in probably the eighteenth century, and has re-established itself in a few locations in Scotland, where there is known to be at least one breeding pair.

Island Wildlife

Scotland's outer islands have their own highly distinctive wildlife. The archipelago of St Kilda was abandoned by humans in 1930 and the **St Kilda house mouse** then died out, alas. The **St Kilda field mouse** has survived well, as has the **St Kilda wren**, a wee bird with a big name: *Troglodytes troglodytes hirtensis*. St Kilda is a UNESCO World Heritage Site, and Europe's most significant seabird colony. It has a large **puffin colony**, the world's largest colony of **gannets** and the largest **fulmar** colony in the British Isles. St Kilda's **Soay sheep** are a very old form of sheep, closely connected to the Mediterranean Mouflon (they may have been brought to St Kilda by Vikings).

Orkney also has a mammal whose origins are mysterious: the **Orkney vole**, whose nearest relations (bafflingly) are in the Balkans (Viking displacement is again a likely explanation). Shetland has over a million breeding seabirds, the highest density of otters in Britain, and the ridiculously cute miniature **Shetland pony** (adult height is between 28 and 42 inches tall), and **Shetland collie**. Shetland is also occasionally visited by Arctic **snowy owls**, one of the world's most striking birds. (Snowy owls bred on the Shetland island of Fetlar from 1967 until 1975.)

Three Domesticated Animals

The most famous domesticated farm animal in Scotland is the **Aberdeen-Angus**, probably the most instantly recognizable species of cattle in the world. The breed was developed in the late nineteenth century from (mainly black) cattle known in the north-east as 'doddies' and hummlies'. Scotland has also produced several species of dogs, including the **West Highland white terrier** and the **Skye terrier**. The Skye terrier's origins are much debated, but something very much like a Skye terrier was described on Skye by the seventeenth century. Greyfriars Bobby was a Skye terrier. Westies are true hunters, originating from tough little dogs bred to hunt otters and foxes. It is said that around 1620 King James VI ordered some 'little white earth dogges' from Argyllshire, and these are – just possibly – the original Westie.

—— Flora ——

Scotland's native trees include oak, fir, larch, Scots pine, hazel, and birch. Scotland is especially rich among nations in the number of 'heritage trees' it has, i.e. trees notable for age, size, or cultural significance. A book could be filled on Scottish trees alone. Grasses are common, and the high regions have heather, ferns (notably bracken), and mosses. Above the 2,000-foot line, the flora becomes alpine, and further up, especially on the harsh Cairngorm country above 3,000 feet, the environment becomes an arctic one. The inland, high ground in Scotland has traditionally been a tough environment for cultivated plants (just about all such species are imports), but (improbable as it may seem) palm trees grow on the west coast, where the Gulf Stream passes.

SEVEN THINGS YOU SHOULD KNOW ABOUT SCOTTISH FLORA

Caledonian Forest: The great Forest of Caledon was famous in Roman times as a source of animals for the arena. The forest was known to the Romans as 'Silva Caledonia' and the huge expanse of trees spread beyond the Empire's frontier to the north of the Tay. What remains is a tiny proportion: 1 per cent of what was once 1.5 million hectares of deep wood. These remnants are very ancient and fragmented. The forest's peak time was probably about 5,000 years ago, with bears, lynx, wolf packs and beaver thriving, and with large wild cattle (aurochs) gathering in the clearings. Farmers began clearing the forest around 4,000 years ago, beginning a process of depletion that continued down through the centuries. By the time the Romans arrived, probably more than half of the forest was already gone. Our ancestors had to make a living somehow, and, as South American farmers do today, the forest was burned back to provide farmland (the oft-repeated story that the Vikings burned the forest down is a myth).

Carrifran Wildwood: The Carrifran Wildwood project was established to create a prehistoric woodland in the Scottish Border hills. The project is based in the beautiful glacial valley of Carrifran, a 1,600-acre valley in the Moffat Hills. There are now more than 400,000 native trees and shrubs in the valley, which now looks pretty much as all the Scottish Border hills and valleys would have done 6,000 years ago.

Fortingall Yew: The village of Fortingall lies within the ancient Pictish heartland of central Scotland, and occupies a strategically important position at the head of Glen Lyon, which is doubtless why the Romans built their still visible camp here (the legend that Pontius Pilate was born in this Roman camp is indeed just a legend, sadly). The name Fortingall supposedly derives from the Gaelic 'Feart nan Gall' – 'Fort of the Strangers'. The great Fortingall yew is in the village churchyard and its age is probably closer to 2,000 years rather than the oft-quoted 5,000, but this still makes it the oldest living thing in Europe.

Heather: Scottish heather is a small shrub which grows on the moors, hills and heath. The plant has been important to the Picts and then Scots in all sorts of ways, from brewing ale to curing the consequent headaches. Heather is an important food source for many animals, including sheep, deer and grouse, and also provides cover for animals. White heather is a traditional lucky charm.

Thistle: The thistle is Scotland's national flower and has all sorts of noble connotations. The origins of the Most Ancient and Noble Order of the Thistle are certainly older than its creation by James VII (the English James II) in 1687. The motto of the order is the famous *Nemo me impune lecessit* – 'No one provokes me with impunity'. The 'Scotch Thistle' is rather brutally classed as a 'noxious weed' in the United States.

Meikleour Beech Hedge: The Meikleour beech hedge has been the world's biggest hedge since 1966: it stands at an average height of 100 feet for a distance of around 600 feet on the Perth to Blairgowrie road. It is said to have been planted in the autumn of 1745 by a lady whose husband was killed at Culloden the following year. Maintained by the Meikleour Trust, the hedge is cut and remeasured every ten years. It looks fabulous in the autumn. Five beeches of note are to be found on Berwick Law; they are the remnant of woodland planted by Sir Hew Dalrymple to commemorate the Act of Union in 1707.

Arran Whitebeam Tree: The Arran whitebeam tree occurs on the island of Arran – and nowhere else in the world. There are two species: the Arran whitebeam (identified in 1897) and the Arran cut-leaved whitebeam (recorded in 1952; it is also known as the bastard mountain ash). There are only a couple of hundred trees of each species in existence, and the two species are classified by the World Wildlife Fund as being dangerously close to extinction.

Scotland has magnificent National Parks, National Nature Reserves (NNRs), RSPB Reserves, and Scottish Wildlife Trust reserves.

The National Parks are **Loch Lomond and the Trossachs** (on Glasgow's doorstep) and the **Cairngorms National Park**. The parks were created by the Scottish parliament in 2002/3 and more will be added. (For our greatest conservationist, John Muir, see The Scots Abroad, p. 244.) NNRs include the haunting gorges of the **Clyde Valley Woodlands**; RSPB reserves include **Lochwinnch** (wetlands, whooper swans, great for kids), **Wood of Cree** (large ancient woodland), **Loch Garten** (ospreys, great all round); Scottish Wildlife Trust Reserves include **Loch of the Lowes** near Dunkeld (ospreys again, lots of events). Check out the webcams!

4

KINGS AND QUEENS

❖

―― The Pictish Monarchs ――

Many of the traditions about Scotland's earliest monarchs are obscure, and often contradictory. The so-called Pictish Chronicle, a list of Pictish kings, apparently dates from the reign of the Scots King Kenneth II, as Kenneth is the last king mentioned. The list we have is a fourteenth-century copy and begins with Drest Son of Erp, who is said to have fought a hundred battles. Historians look for independent confirmation of the existence of these kings before accepting them as actual rulers, using sources such as the *Annals of Ulster* and the *Anglo-Saxon Chronicles*.

One of the most famous of the Pictish kings is King Bridei, whom Columba travelled to see around 563 (see p. 129). The account of the trip was written a hundred years later by Columba's biographer Adamnan. Bridei's home was possibly a small fort on the site of the present Inverness Castle, or maybe on a ridge overlooking the Beauly Firth. The confusion that surrounds the Picts in popular culture is well illustrated by a Victorian painting by William Hole in the Scottish National Portrait Gallery, which depicts Columba preaching to Bridei. As Lloyd Laing points out in his *Celtic Britain* (1979), the work is a patchwork of anachronism, a mixture of elements diverse in time and space: Bridei wears a second-century armlet, an eighth-century AD brooch and an eighth-century BC Italian helmet, while one of Columba's team carries a twelfth-century crozier. Yet, as Laing says, it all looks just fine to us.

—— Scottish Kings and Queens ——

KENNETH MACALPIN (reigned 840–58)

The *Dictionary of National Biography* says that MacAlpin was king of the Dalriadan Scots from 840 and ruler of the Picts from 842. Other historians say he should be regarded as a late Pictish king and not the first Scottish king, though his descendants became Scottish kings. There is a later tradition that MacAlpin invited the Pictish nobility to a council and killed them all ('the treachery of Scone'). MacAlpin was succeeded by his brother **Donald I** (860–2), then by his two sons: **Constantine I** (863–77), nicknamed 'the Wine-bountiful', and **Aed** (877–8), nicknamed 'Aed of the White Flowers'. These were the dual progenitors of the Scots royal line. Their lines of descent produced kings for close to 150 years, after a pause for: **Giric** (*c.*878–89) and/or **Eochaid** (878–89), who are at best obscure and possibly apocryphal. **Donald II** (889–900), the son of Constantine I, was nicknamed 'the Madman', and was succeeded by Aed's son **Constantine II** (900–43). During his long Viking-plagued reign, the realm was now generally known as 'Scotland' (at last). Unusually for a king of his time and lineage, he abdicated to become a monk and possibly even died in bed. **Malcolm I** (943–54), nicknamed 'the Dangerous Red', was the son of Donald II and Constantine II's cousin, and was succeeded by Constantine II's son Indulf (954–62), nicknamed 'the Aggressor'. Then came **Dub** or **Duff** (962–7), son of Malcolm I, nicknamed 'the Vehement', and then **Cuilen** (967–71), son of Indulf, nicknamed 'the White'. Next was **Kenneth II** (971–95), son of Malcolm I; nicknamed 'the

Fratricide', he raided into Strathclyde, Northumbria, and as far south as Cheshire. According to one chronicle, Kenneth acknowledged the overlordship of the English king, Edgar the Peaceable. The Anglo-Scottish border was also becoming defined at this time. His successor was **Constantine III** (995–7), son of Cuilen, nicknamed 'the Bald' according to one source, the last of the line of Aed. Then came **Kenneth III** (997–1005), son of Dub. Nicknamed 'the Brown', or 'the Chief', he was killed in battle by Malcolm II.

MALCOLM II (1005–34)

Many lists of Scottish royals begin with Malcolm II: we are now entering familiar historical territory, with no more obscure Constantines or Girics. Malcolm, a son of Kenneth II, got the throne by killing Kenneth III. Malcolm's nickname was 'the Destroyer' and he was notable even in Scottish history for dealing lethally with potential enemies. He invaded England but was forced to submit to the Danish King of England, Cnut (Canute), in 1031.

DUNCAN I (1034–40)

Son of an abbot called Crinan and one of Malcolm II's daughters, Duncan's nickname was 'the Diseased'. The historical Duncan bears little resemblance to Shakespeare's noble old man. This Duncan was a young, vigorous warrior, born into a world of succession wars worthy of the New Jersey mafia; his mother was possibly married to both an Earl of Orkney and the King of Moray before wedding her abbot – Moray was Macbeth's home ground. Duncan led a disastrous raid into England in 1039 which came to a shuddering halt at Durham; the following year he led an army into Moray and was killed fighting Macbeth's warriors.

MACBETH (1040–57)

King of Moray, and possibly a grandson of Malcolm II, Macbeth grabbed the throne by defeating and killing Duncan. His nickname was 'the Red King'. Again, the character of Macbeth and the nature of his reign were quite different from the Shakespeare version. The eleventh century was a tough time to be a Scottish monarch. Apart from incessant struggle against rival claimants to the throne, and with many minor powers all with quite literal axes to grind, the kingdom also lay open to attacks from the Orkney Vikings in the north (though Earl Thorfinn was an ally of Macbeth's, such alliances dissolved easily), and from the Northumbrian kingdom in the south. (The novelist Dorothy Dunnett proposed a fascinating theory in her novel *King Hereafter*, in which she suggested that Thorfinn and Macbeth were the same person: that the pagan Thorfinn became the Christian Macbeth on baptism.)

Macbeth made at least one pilgrimage to Rome, to see Pope Leo IX. It may seem odd to think of Macbeth as a player on the European stage, never mind visiting the Pope, but such was the case. Europe was undergoing dramatic shifts of power; the pathways of dynastic struggle ran up and down the Atlantic coast and across the North Sea as well as by land, and Scotland was by no means a negligible state. Macbeth was the first, but not the last, Scottish monarch to take Norman knights into his service. And his rule was popular. Thanks to his deals, promises and threats, the realm lived free from war.

Macbeth had a good innings for a medieval Scottish king, reigning for seventeen years before being killed in battle against Duncan's son, Malcolm III, in 1057. Scottish history subsequently began again to resemble a series of *The Sopranos*, with Macbeth's rule being looked back to as a time of peace and plenty.

LULACH (1057–8)

Lulach was Macbeth's stepson, nicknamed 'the Unfortunate' or 'the Foolish'. In an obscure development – Lulach's father had been killed by Macbeth and it is possible the son fought in alliance with Malcolm – Lulach took the throne after his stepfather's death. It was a short reign: Malcolm ambushed and killed him in 1058.

MALCOLM III (1058–93)

Son of Duncan I. His famous nickname of 'Canmore' or 'Big Head' may have originally belonged to his great-grandson Malcolm IV. His second wife Margaret is the only Scottish royal saint, Saint Margaret of Scotland; Margaret was born in Hungary, the grand-niece of an English saint, Edward the Confessor. William the Conqueror, after destroying much of northern England, met Malcolm at Abernethy and accepted his submission. After William Rufus took the English throne, Malcolm launched several raids into the English north-east, the last one notable for being so brutal it shocked even the warlords of his day. He was killed in battle at Alnwick.

DONALD III (1093–7)

Like Malcolm, Donald was a son of Duncan I. His nickname was 'Donal Bane', 'Donald the Fair'. He seized the throne in the chaos after Malcolm's death and was himself briefly deposed in 1094 by his nephew, **Duncan II**, a son of Malcolm III who was killed shortly after being enthroned. Donald was murdered in 1097.

EDGAR (1097–1107)

Son of Malcolm III and the sainted Margaret, Edgar's nickname was 'the Valiant'. Edgar's disputed claim to the throne was decisively supported by William Rufus. The *Dictionary of National Biography* records that Edgar gave the King of Munster a large animal – a camel or elephant – which is not that implausible since there were many Scots in the First Crusade of 1098–9. Ailred, Abbot of Rievaulx, described Edgar as 'sweet and loveable'. He never married, had no known children, and died peacefully in Edinburgh.

ALEXANDER I (1107–24)

Alexander was the fifth son of Malcolm III and Margaret, and may have been named after Pope Alexander II. His nature was a dangerous blend of piety and bloodlust, and his nickname was 'the Fierce'. He had a troubled relationship with both his brother David, who succeeded him, and the Church, and fought beside the English King Henry I against the Welsh in 1114. Abbot Ailred described Alexander as 'beyond measure awesome to his subjects'. He died in his court at Stirling.

DAVID I (1124–53)

The youngest son of Malcolm III; his nickname was 'the Holy'. He had lived at the English court as a child. Scotland during his reign has been described as undergoing a 'Davidian revolution' which included more feudalism, Norman influence, over a dozen new monasteries and the foundation of burghs. He also introduced Scotland's first coinage.

MALCOLM IV (1153–65)

Grandson of David I; his nickname was 'the Virgin', or 'Malcolm the Maiden'. This nickname did not imply weakness; after crushing a Moray rebel he displaced the entire population. It is now believed he was the original 'Malcolm Canmore' and that this designation was projected backwards on to his great-grandfather, Malcolm III. Malcolm died prematurely aged twenty-four at Jedburgh. He may have suffered from bone deformation (Paget's disease). He never married.

WILLIAM I (1165–1214)

Brother of Malcolm IV, his nicknames were 'the Lion' and 'the Rough'. His lion banner became Scotland's royal standard. William was a physically imposing man with perhaps too much disregard for his own safety: he charged an English army at the Battle of Alnwick (1174), was unhorsed, and captured. Despite such impetuosity his reign was a long one. He swore fealty to the English King Henry II in 1175, and died peacefully in Stirling in his early seventies.

ALEXANDER II (1214–49)

Son of William I, he seems to have had no nickname. He supported the English barons in their war against King John. His campaign was a notable one, in that his troops reached Dover and returned again without having been defeated (or, in truth, having had to fight). He died on the small Hebridean island of Kerrera, on his way to assert his authority in the Western Isles.

ALEXANDER III (1249–86)

The son of Alexander II, he became king at the age of eight. After the Battle of Largs and the failure of the Norwegian expedition, Alexander established a theoretical Scottish rule in the Western Isles (Norway still held Orkney and Shetland). He gave the title 'Lord of the Isles' to the MacDonalds, the clan rewarding him by becoming virtually independent rulers. He died from injuries sustained by falling off a horse. With hindsight, Alexander's reign was considered as a time of peace and prosperity:

When Alexander our King was dead,
That Scotland led in love and le [law],
Away was wealth of ale and bread,
Of wine and wax, of game and glee.
Our gold was changed into lead –
Christ born into virginity,
Succour Scotland and remedy
Which placèd is in perplexity.

MARGARET (1286–90)

Margaret – the 'Maid of Norway' – was the daughter of King Eric II of Norway and Alexander III's daughter (also called Margaret). She gained the throne at the age of three and was never crowned, indeed never set foot in Scotland. She died aged seven (in Orkney) on her way to Scotland and is buried in Bergen.

A marriage between Margaret and the English King Edward I's son Edward had been agreed. Despite Mel Gibson's 'English Go Home' speech in *Braveheart*, the kingdoms had been at peace with each other for most of the thirteenth century, with thousands of English and Scots heading over the border in both directions to settle in harmony. This ended in 1296.

INTERREGNUM (1290–92)

JOHN BALLIOL (1292–6)

Balliol was a great-great-great-grandson of David I, and was enthroned at Scone in 1292. King Edward I regularly challenged John's authority. Edward (who became known as the 'Hammer of the Scots') invaded in 1296, thus bringing to an end the long peace between England and Scotland and inaugurating what became known as the 'Scottish Wars of

Independence'. He imprisoned John 1296–9, then transferred him into papal custody. John died in Helicourt, France, c.1314.

INTERREGNUM (1296–1306)

ROBERT I (1306–29)

Robert the Bruce (Robert de Brus) was of Norman ancestry on his father's side, and Scots on his mother's side. He was the great-great-great-great-grandson of David I and therefore believed he had a claim to the Scottish throne. He was a distant relative of Balliol but supported Edward I against his kinsman. Despite swearing allegiance to Edward in 1296, Bruce took part in the independence war against the English, and, in the manner of the time, devastated the lands of those who stuck to their oaths to Edward, though he reaffirmed his oath to Edward in 1297. Following the Battle of Stirling Bridge, Bruce again switched sides, but when Edward defeated the Scots at the Battle of Falkirk, Bruce's land somehow escaped seizure (Edward likely regarded Bruce as a power who could be bought and sold at will). William Wallace resigned as 'Guardian of Scotland' after Falkirk (Edward executed him in 1305), and Bruce and a nobleman called John Comyn (the 'Red Comyn') became joint Guardians. This arrangement ended with Bruce stabbing Comyn before the high altar of a monastery in Dumfries: Comyn survived the stabbing, but Bruce's henchmen finished him off. The Pope then excommunicated first Bruce, then all of Scotland. Bruce was crowned at Scone in 1306, but eventually had to flee to Rathlin Island, off the Ulster coast (he may or may not have shared his cave with a spider). Bruce returned to Scotland in 1307. The Scottish Wars of Independence were also civil wars in Scotland, with Bruce winning the big prize. This victory came at a terrible cost to the people of the Comyn lands in particular, who suffered a devastation by Bruce's forces in 1308, long remembered as the Harrying or Herschip (Hardship) of Buchan. This was medieval war at its most brutal, with terrible consequences for the people of northeast Scotland. Edward died, was succeeded by his less soldierly son Edward II, and Bruce returned to the fray, in 1314 inflicting a stunning defeat on the English at Bannockburn. Bruce died in Cardross in 1329, of what has been described as 'unclean ailment' – possibly leprosy, though syphilis has also been proposed.

DAVID II (1329–71)
Son of Robert the Bruce, he became king at the age of five, having been married the previous year to Joan, youngest daughter of Edward II; she bore the lovely nickname of 'Joan of the Tower'. David was taken prisoner by the English at the Battle of Neville's Cross in 1346 and was held in England for eleven years. He and Joan had no children. Joan died aged forty-one in 1362, and David died in Edinburgh Castle in 1371, aged forty-six.

ROBERT II (1371–90)
Robert was the grandson of Robert I, and was enthroned at Scone after the death of David II. He was known as the 'Steward', a designation that eventually gave its name to the royal house of Stewart. He had around twenty-three children, most of them legitimate, and bequeathed through them much dispute about rights of succession. He seems otherwise to have been a fairly remote monarch and was not present at the Battle of Otterburn. He died at Dundonald in 1390.

ROBERT III (1390–1406)
The eldest son of Robert II (by one of Robert's mistresses, whom he subsequently married), Robert III was enthroned in

1390, and his reign was plagued by half-brother conspiracies. The Scottish nobles exploited his problems gleefully. Robert sent his young son James into hiding, quite rightly fearing for the boy's life. James ended up in English captivity and Robert died soon after in 1406 at Rothesay Castle, of grief it was said. One source also claims that he asked to be buried in a midden (dunghill) with the epitaph, 'Here lies the worst of kings and most miserable of men'. He was buried at Scone instead.

James I (1406–37)

The son of Robert III, James was imprisoned by the English for eighteen years from 1406 to 1424. The captivity was not too terrible – the English King Henry IV had him educated and kept in comfort – and being kept away from Scotland almost certainly saved his life. Scotland paid the huge ransom of £40,000 demanded by Henry VI, and James returned to a faction-ridden Scotland with his English bride, Joan (none of the five Scottish kings called James would wed a Scots-born woman). James was finally enthroned in 1424. He was assassinated by a group of nobles in 1437, and was buried in the Carthusian Priory in Perth.

James II (1437–60)

The son of James I, James II was seven when he gained the throne after his father's murder. His nickname was 'Fiery Face' thanks to a scarlet birthmark, but the nickname may also refer to his aggressive nature. He fought long and hard against the Douglasses, and was reprimanded by his own parliament for his high-handed behaviour. He didn't care for golf (as it interfered with archery practice), demanding that the game be 'utterly cryt downe and nocht usyt'. He was a noted exponent of modern artillery, and died at the siege of Roxburgh in 1460, when one of his siege cannons blew up, killing him on the spot.

James III (1460–88)

The son of James II, James III was enthroned in 1460, aged about eight. He was not a popular monarch, and nor does he seem to have been as cultured a man as later chronicles suggested (with some disdain). Amid much factional struggle (most notably with the fractious Boyd family), James married Margaret of Denmark in 1469, and Scotland finally achieved sovereignty over Orkney and Shetland. He was killed at the Battle of Sauchieburn in 1488, fighting against rebellious Scots nobles who claimed to be fighting on behalf of his son, James.

James IV (1488–1513)

The son of James III, James IV was enthroned at Scone aged sixteen, and was appalled to learn that his father's killers claimed to have been fighting for him. He wore a heavy chain in penance (under his clothes) at Lent for the rest of his life. Regarded as an effective leader, he made peace with England by marrying Margaret, daughter of Henry VII – which led in the next century to James VI becoming king of both countries. He made four trips around the Western Isles, to assert royal authority over the Hebrides ('the Daunting of the Isles'). James is seen as a fine example of a Renaissance prince. The Spanish ambassador records that James spoke Latin ('very well'), French, German, Flemish, Italian, Spanish, and Gaelic. James was a great sponsor of the arts, the composer Robert Carver and the renowned poet William Dunbar being two of many people who benefited from his patronage. His reign ended in disaster, however – at Flodden.

James V (1513–42)

The son of James IV, he inherited the throne at the age of one when his father died at Flodden. In 1525 his stepfather, the Earl of Angus, imprisoned him; James escaped in 1528, and proscribed Angus (and the Douglasses) from coming within 7 miles of him. He followed his father in making sure that the Lords of the Isles knew their place (Portree – 'Port of the king' – on Skye, takes its name from his visit in 1540, along with several warships). When news of the birth of his only child, Mary, was brought to him on his deathbed, he is supposed to have said, 'It came with a lass and it will end with a lass', a reference to the origin of the House of Stewart through Marjorie, daughter of Robert I. In fact, it didn't end with Mary, but with Queen Anne, the last Stewart monarch, who reigned from 1702 to 1714.

MARY, QUEEN OF SCOTS OR MARY I (1542–67)

The most famous of all Scottish monarchs, the six-day-old Mary inherited the throne on the death of her father in 1542 (her mother was Mary of Guise and she was also briefly Queen Consort of France, 1559–60). She was sent to France in 1548 to marry the French dauphin and thus give new life to the 'Auld Alliance' between Scotland and France against the English: an alliance that now had a religious dimension, two Catholic countries against the Protestant, heretic English (in France Mary adopted the French spelling 'Stuart' for 'Stewart', a form retained by succeeding royals). The dauphin died and Mary returned in 1561 to a Scotland in which Protestants were on the rise. Mary proved tolerant in rule.

In 1565 she married her Catholic cousin Darnley, a brutal man who murdered Mary's secretary David Rizzio in front of her; she was then six months pregnant with the future James VI, who was baptized a Catholic, thus further outraging John Knox and other Protestant clerics. They were already denouncing Mary in the strongest terms, not just for attending mass, but for taking part in sinful pastimes such as dancing. Darnley was murdered in 1567, and a few months later Mary married the man widely believed to have killed him, the Earl of Bothwell. Bothwell had abducted Mary before the marriage and allegedly raped her, thus forcing her to marry him.

The Scottish nobles formed an alliance against Mary and Bothwell, and Mary was imprisoned in Loch Leven Castle in 1567, where she miscarried twins, and was forced to abdicate in favour of James (who was one year old). Mary escaped, and launched a war against the nobles, which ended in defeat at the Battle of Langside in 1568. She fled to England, where Queen Elizabeth had her imprisoned for nineteen years in various castles. Mary became – wittingly or unwittingly – the focus of Catholic plots against Elizabeth, and eventually Mary was executed at Fotheringhay Castle in 1587. (Bothwell had died in a Danish dungeon in 1578, after ten years of harsh imprisonment.)

JAMES VI OF SCOTLAND AND I OF ENGLAND
(Scottish reign: 1567–1625; Joint reign: 1603–25)

James became King of Scotland aged one, and King of England aged thirty-six. His early life was a traumatic one, his kingdom was riven by factional and religious strife, and his mother was executed in England for treason in 1587. He denounced the execution as 'preposterous and strange' but the following year – the year of the Spanish Armada – he pledged Elizabeth his support against the Spanish as 'your natural son'. When Elizabeth died on 24 March 1603, James was proclaimed King of England in London a few hours later. He proclaimed himself 'King of Great Britain' in 1605. Though initially very popular, enthusiasm for James soon dimmed; his favourites were scorned, and his practice of selling honours for cash was also loathed (knighthoods initially cost £40 but were so popular he raised the price to £100).

In 1605 the Gunpowder Plot was discovered, and Guy Fawkes was arrested in the cellar beneath the House of Lords with a ton of gunpowder at his back. He was taken to King James's bedchamber at one o'clock in the morning where he calmly said that he wanted to kill the king and destroy parliament. James asked Fawkes why he was so keen on killing him, and Fawkes replied that the king had been excommunicated by the Pope, and that dangerous diseases required 'desperate remedies'. Showing that he was an English patriot as well as a Catholic, Fawkes told James and his court that one of his aims had been to 'blow the Scots back to Scotland', a detail that was suppressed as it would have encouraged sympathy for Fawkes among the English, many of whom regarded the Scots who accompanied James as a corrupt and unsavoury lot. Fawkes's one regret was that the scheme failed.

James gave permission for torture to be used on Fawkes, instructing the interrogators thus: 'The gentler tortours are to be first used unto him, et sic per gradus ad maiora tenditur [and thus by steps extended to greater ones], and so God speed your good work.' After Fawkes's execution, James then confirmed his public reputation for cowardice by going into seclusion for a while.

When Pocahontas and her husband came to London in 1617, they were introduced to King James at a Ben Jonson masque (at which she was given a royal seat). The Pocahontas party were told they had just been introduced to the king, and Pocahontas expressed some surprise that such a man could be King of England, an opinion that was increasingly expressed among the English as well. This occasion seems at least to have been reasonably sober; at another masque, Queen Anne's ladies were too drunk to stand and one spilt custard all over James.

James was probably homosexual, or at least more interested in young men than women. He was undoubtedly an intellectual, but also credulous: his belief in witchcraft was a malign influence on both kingdoms. Sir Antony Weldon described him thus (in 1651): 'A very wise man was wont to say that he believed him the wisest fool in Christendom, meaning him wise in small things, but a fool in weighty affairs.' By the end of his reign, tensions between king and parliament were growing, and his son, Charles I, was executed by his subjects in 1649, after a civil war that changed the world for ever.

THE JACOBITE CHALLENGE, 1689–1746

The term 'Jacobite' derives from the Latin 'Jacobus' – James – and was applied to anyone working to restore the deposed James (VII of Scotland, II of England, brother of Charles II) and his dynasty to the throne of England, Wales, Scotland and Ireland, and in doing so depose William and Mary and their heirs, who took the throne in 1689. James was a Roman Catholic and had not been wanted as king by large numbers of the English or the Scots. Many Anglicans, however, no matter how anti-Catholic, found themselves in a bind: James was the anointed king and to accept his overthrow was to accept that there was no 'divine right' of kings to govern, and there was wide-ranging (if muted) sympathy for the Jacobite cause in England.

In Scotland, the seventeenth century had been a bloody one and the crisis of 1689 saw fierce fighting between Williamite (mainly Lowland) and Highland Jacobite forces. The Jacobites, led by Claverhouse, 'Bluidy Clavers' (subsequently dubbed 'Bonnie Dundee' by Walter Scott) won at Killiecrankie:

> I fought at land, I fought at sea
> At hame I fought my auntie-o

> But I met the Devil and Dundee
> On the braes o' Killiecrankie-o.

But 'Clavers' was killed along with 2,000 others during the battle, and the Jacobites lost the rematch at Dunkeld. The next Jacobite rising in Scotland came in 1715 – the '15. The aim of the '15 was to place the 'Old Pretender', James II's son (James Francis Edward Stuart, 1688–1766) on the throne. Sympathetic clans were raised, JFES landed in Scotland, and fought an indecisive battle at Sheriffmuir, where, as a contemporary ballad cheerfully put it:

> And we ran, and they ran,
> And they ran, and we ran.

Detecting a lack of enthusiasm for the cause, JFES abandoned plans for a coronation at Scone and returned to France.

The '45 was a more protracted affair. Charles Edward Stuart (1720–88), the Old Pretender's son, landed at Glenfinnan, raised the clans, and marched on London, reaching as far south as Derby before deciding to retreat. The '45 ended at Culloden and Charlie went on the run, helped in his final escape by Flora MacDonald.

Arguably, one of the major problems for the Jacobites was their Highland power base: being able to raise a Highland army was one thing, advancing with that army into the south was quite another. In any case, the waverers and the calculators outweighed the die-hards on either side. At Sheriffmuir, Rob Roy and a detachment of MacGregors hung about on the wings and could have swung the battle either way, but stayed aloof (Rob was quite rightly distrusted by both sides).

In 1745, that dreadful old Highland rogue Lord Lovat could have made a decisive impact on the campaign. Lovat was as much a London player as he was a Highland one, and if he had thrown his full, deadly weight behind Charlie then the outcome could have been very different. Lovat dithered too long and ended up losing his head for treason. The Jacobite challenge needed luck and shrewdness, but had neither.

A NOTE ON FLORA

Flora MacDonald was briefly imprisoned in London and released in 1747 to universal acclaim: London sympathizers raised over £1,500 for her. In 1773 Flora and her husband Allan received Boswell and Johnson on Skye, Johnson saying of her that her name 'will be mentioned in history, and if courage and fidelity be virtues, mentioned with honour'. In 1774 Flora emigrated to North Carolina and when the rebellion broke out, raised Highland troops to fight for King George. Like many other Loyalists, Flora and Allan suffered badly in the aftermath of the rebel victory, and they returned to Skye, where Flora died in 1790, aged sixty-eight.

5

Politics and Government

❖

The 1707 Union of the Scottish and English Parliaments

From 1603, England and Scotland became united under one monarch. The union of the crowns was, to everyone's relief, a peaceful resolution to the English succession problem. James grew more unpopular as his reign went on, but most people's expectations were that the structures of governance would continue much as before. However, the rest of the seventeenth century turned out to be turbulent, with the Thirty Years War in Europe; in Britain, Charles I was executed, and a republic established in England, the 'natural' orders of succession and authority were shaken to their foundations, and the 'divine right' of kings to govern became a highly problematic belief.

A union of the parliaments was always possible, and on 16 January 1707 the Scottish parliament voted to agree to a union with England; the Act of Union agreed by both parliaments came into force on 1 May 1707, with Scotland keeping its separate legal and religious traditions. The new parliament was called the 'Parliament of Great Britain', and there followed desultory attempts throughout the eighteenth century to call England 'South Britain', which everybody ignored, and Scotland 'North Britain'; the latter term achieved some partial recognition but gradually faded into a merited oblivion.

For many Scots, the Earl of Seafield summed up their feelings by touching the royal assent to union with the royal sceptre, and saying, 'There's an end of an auld sang.' Others saw it as a tragic betrayal of Scottish nationhood: there were riots in Glasgow and Edinburgh. As Robert Burns later put it, in tones of high indignation:

> The English steel we could disdain,
> Secure in valour's station;
> But English gold has been our bane –
> Such a parcel of rogues in a nation!

In truth, the Scottish MPs were probably no more or less corrupt or unprincipled than politicians at any period. And with the coming of the Scottish Enlightenment and the Industrial Revolution, deep resentment at the Union largely became the preserve of poets, the occasional mob, and also outraged members of the Church of Scotland who could no longer burn witches after 1736. See The Law of the Land: Witch Hunt: Janet Horne is condemned to be burned alive, p. 80.

——Scottish Prime Ministers of Great Britain ——

BORN IN SCOTLAND
John Stuart, 3rd Earl of Bute (1762–3, Tory): born in Edinburgh

George Hamilton-Gordon, 4th Earl of Aberdeen (1852–5, Tory): born in Edinburgh

Arthur Balfour (1902–5, Tory): born in Whittingehame

Henry Campbell-Bannerman (1905–8, Liberal): born in Glasgow

James Ramsay MacDonald (1929–35, Labour): born in Lossiemouth

Tony Blair (1997–2007, Labour): born in Edinburgh

Gordon Brown (2007–, Labour): born in Glasgow

BORN ELSEWHERE (BUT STILL SCOTTISH)
Archibald Primrose, 5th Earl of Rosebery (1894–5, Liberal): born in London

Andrew Bonar Law (1922–3, Unionist): born in New Brunswick, Canada

Harold Macmillan (1957–63, Tory): born in London

Alec Douglas-Home (1963–4, Tory): born in London

(Several other PMs, such as Asquith, were not Scottish but represented Scottish constituencies.)

—— Some Notable Scots MPs ——

Duchess of Atholl (1874–1960): Conservative MP for Kinross and West Perthshire, 1923–38 (nickname: 'The Red Duchess'); first Tory female minister, 1924–9

Willie Gallacher (1881–1965): Communist Party MP for West Fife, 1935–50

Edwin Scrymgeour (1866–1947): Britain's only prohibitionist MP (for the Scottish Prohibition Party), 1922–31, defeated Winston Churchill in Dundee

James Keir Hardie (1856–1915): founder of the Independent Labour Party and MP for West Ham, 1892–5; for Merthyr Tydfil, 1900–15

The **West Lothian Question** (as it was dubbed by Enoch Powell) was asked by Tam Dalyell (Labour MP for West Lothian) on November 1977, in reaction to talk of devolution:

> For how long will English constituencies and English Honourable members tolerate… at least 119 Honourable Members from Scotland, Wales and Northern Ireland exercising an important, and probably often decisive, effect on British politics while they themselves have no say in the same matters in Scotland, Wales and Northern Ireland?

The West Lothian Question seemed at the time to be of great constitutional import and no one has ever had an answer to it except for Lord Irvine, who suggested in 1998 that the answer to the question was to stop asking it – which is what has happened. Unlike the Schleswig-Holstein Question, everyone understands the West Lothian Question, but few now care about the answer – if there is one.

The UK Scotland Act 1978 set out plans for a devolved legislative assembly for Scotland, but with the requirement that the people of Scotland be asked if they actually wanted the devolved assembly or not. The referendum on devolution was held in 1979 and asked the Scottish electorate to answer 'yes' or 'no' to the question: 'Do you want the provisions of the Scotland Act to be put into effect?'

The referendum had a creditable 63.8 per cent turnout, and the result was:

> YES – 51.6 per cent (1,230,937 votes)
> NO – 48.4 per cent (1,153,500 votes)

This small majority for devolution was not enough, however, as the government had controversially required that at least 40 per cent of the electorate should turn out to vote yes. The turnout was excellent, but not sufficient, and many supporters of devolution felt cheated.

THE COMING OF DEVOLUTION

The question was asked again in 1997, but without the daft 40 per cent qualification. And the result of the referendum on 11 September 1997 (turnout 60.4 per cent) to the proposition, 'I agree that there should be a Scottish Parliament', was:

> YES – 74.3 per cent (1,775,045 votes)
> NO – 25.7 per cent (614,000 votes)

To the accompanying proposition, 'I agree that a Scottish Parliament should have tax-varying powers', the result was:

> YES – 63.5 per cent (1,512,889 votes)
> NO – 36.5 per cent (870,263 votes)

Scotland's devolved parliament was officially opened on 1 July 1999. There was near universal consensus among Scottish political parties (except the Tories) that some form of devolution was both inevitable and indeed desirable: for the clear majority of politicians and 'opinion formers', the devolution process represented the 'settled will' of the Scottish people. For unionists, devolution was seen as a last stage of government with fiddly details to be sorted out over the years. For nationalists, devolution was regarded as the first major step towards independence.

Three politicians did most to bring about devolution:

John Smith (1938–1994): Scottish Labour politician and Labour leader, 1992–4. John Smith was an ardent supporter of devolution, which he saw as necessary to strengthen British democracy. His death in 1994 from a heart attack gave a huge impetus to the proponents of the devolution cause. In the House of Commons in May 1999, on the eve of the first Scottish parliamentary election (held on 6 May) for around 300 years, Prime Minister Tony Blair said:

> A Scottish Parliament was called 'unfinished business' by John Smith. There is no better expression of his values and his love of democracy than the Scottish Parliament. It does offer us the chance of an enhanced and strengthened United Kingdom in which those things which are distinctively Scottish can be handled in Scotland and those things where it is right that we co-operate and work in partnership, we do so within the United Kingdom.

In a fitting coincidence, the new Scottish parliament met for the first time on the fifth anniversary of John Smith's death.

Donald Dewar *(1937–2000)*: Appointed Secretary of State for Scotland in 1997, Dewar set himself the task of turning John Smith's devolution dream into reality. The Labour Party failed to achieve an outright majority in the 1999 election, and formed a coalition with the Liberal Democrats, with Dewar becoming First Minister. He died of heart failure in 2000. His statue stands at the top of Buchanan Street in Glasgow, with his words introducing the Parliament Act of 1998 engraved beneath him: 'There shall be a Scottish Parliament'.

Alex Salmond *(1954–)*: Scottish Nationalist MP, leader of the SNP from 1990 to 2000 and again from 2004; having stood down as leader in 2000, he surprised everybody, not least his own party, by standing for election again in 2004. A highly regarded economist (and racing tipster), Salmond threw his considerable political weight behind the campaign for a devolved parliament, while being perfectly open about his perception of the devolved parliament as a stepping stone to full independence. On 16 May 2007 the SNP won the Scottish parliament election with forty-seven seats (one more than Labour). Salmond became First Minister, and the leader of the SNP minority government. After the Referendum defeat he resigned as SNP leader and became an MP in 2015.

The 'No' Campaign
The campaign against devolution was led by the 'Think Twice' campaign. The campaign, which drew most of its support from the Scottish Tories, was a total failure, and may even have had the effect of persuading wavering Scots to vote in favour of devolution, rather than against it.

The Parliament Building
The Scottish parliament building was designed by Catalan architect Enrico Miralles (who died in 2000) and cost £414 million to build (ten times the original estimate), and seemed on occasion to be much more controversial than the actual fact of devolution itself. Miralles said he wanted to create a building that looked as if it were 'growing out of the land'. Admirers described the building as unique and one that would attract many visitors; non-admirers described it as just another 'signature' building of the sort that many cities now build. Some of the structure's critics – such as Margo MacDonald MSP – claimed that it was not particularly eco-friendly and would be difficult to maintain. Her words rang true when parliamentary proceedings had to be abandoned in March 2006 when a 12-foot beam came loose in the debating chamber. The debating chamber is semicircular, in the hope, it was said, that

the design would encourage constructive debate, rather than the confrontational atmosphere claimed to be fostered by the opposing benches of the Westminster parliament. These 'constructive debates' can be watched from a visitors' gallery.

HOW THE SCOTTISH PARLIAMENT WORKS: DEVOLVED AND NON-DEVOLVED MATTERS

Devolution means the delegation of certain powers from UK government at Westminster to the Scottish Executive at Holyrood (the SNP rebranded 'Executive' as 'Government' in 2007, a change now regarded by all as both appropriate and lasting).

The Scottish Government is a different beast from the Scottish parliament (basically the same as the relation between the UK government and UK parliament).

The Scottish Government consists of:

- **a First Minister:** the First Minister is Scotland's version of the UK Prime Minister; they appoint the ministerial team and decide their responsibilities

- **the Scottish law officers,** who are the Lord Advocate and the Solicitor General: they advise the Scottish Executive on legal matters and represent its interests in court (and do not need to be MSPs)

- **Cabinet secretaries and their ministers:** Cabinet secretaries are assisted by the ministers who have specific responsibilities (e.g. justice, health, education), and their function is to develop and implement legislation and policy in their assigned areas.

The Scottish parliament has the right to make laws on matters such as education, health and housing, which are defined as 'devolved matters'. The devolved matters are listed in 2008 as:

- agriculture, forestry and fishing
- education and training
- environment
- Gaelic
- health
- housing
- law and home affairs
- local government
- natural and built heritage
- planning
- police and fire services
- social work
- sport and the arts
- statistics and public records
- tourism and economic development
- transport

In fact, many of these devolved matters are up for debate. See, for example, the controversy over the 'Lockerbie Bomber' case: *HM Advocate v. Megrahi* (2000). As for planning, controversy tends to drip 'down' to the council level, rather than 'up' to the UK government level: thus the Scottish Government decided to review and decide on the American tycoon Donald Trump's plans to build a golf course and housing development in Scotland, after an Aberdeenshire planning committee rejected it (see p. 159).

The UK government decides on 'reserved matters'. These include foreign affairs, defence, social security, and anything deemed to have a constitutional impact.

One of the reserved matters that continually erupts into controversy is fisheries policy, and the SNP regularly insists that

Scotland's fishing fleet would be allowed to catch more fish if the Executive were allowed to argue on their behalf.

The UK parliament has the right to make laws on any subject that applies to Scotland, but will 'not normally' pass such legislation without the consent of the Scottish parliament.

The Holyrood election of 2011 produced a result that the voting system was supposed to prevent: an overall majority for one party.

The Scottish voting system gives the voter two votes: the constituency vote is as Westminster, first past the post (aka winner takes all); but the second regional vote, which elects another 56 MSPs, is designed to take into account the amount of votes cast for each party or individual, thus ensuring a fairer representation in parliament.

The Labour Party had gradually come to be seen as the 'natural party of government' in Scotland. In 2011, however, the SNP swept to power on a huge wave of popular support, taking 69 seats; Labour 37, Tories 15, LibDems 5, Greens 2, Independent 1 (the redoubtable, and sadly missed Margo MacDonald).

This thumping victory led to a referendum on Scottish independence, a referendum long anticipated by nationalists. The referendum was held on 18 September 2014, and asked the question: 'Should Scotland be an independent country?' The result was

NO – 2,001,926 (55.3%)
YES – 1,617,989 (44.7%)

The turnout was 84.6%, the highest percentage recorded for any election (or referendum) in the UK since universal suffrage began.

So that was apparently that. The leader of the SNP – Alex Salmond – resigned, making way for his deputy, Nicola Sturgeon. One Labour MP suggested that the SNP would have fewer seats than the Tories in the coming General Election in May 2015. The election, however, saw the SNP almost sweep the board in Scotland; 56 out of 59 MPs, with Labour, Tories and LibDems getting one apiece. In one of the most remarkable victories achieved in modern politics anywhere, the SNP gained 50 seats, and Sturgeon herself attained quite phenomenal personal approval ratings. The debate over independence continues.

The run up to the Holyrood election of May 2016 was described as 'boring' by many, yet turned out to be anything but. Nicola Sturgeon led the SNP to a third term in government, Labour crashed, and the Tories staged an astonishing comeback, replacing Labour as the biggest opposition party. The final tally for constituency and region seats was 63 for SNP, 31 Tory, 24 Labour, 6 Green, and 5 LibDems. The SNP were two seats short of the 65 needed to retain the overall majority they had in the last parliament.

The 'Leave or Remain' EU Referendum of 23 June 2016 showed a deep divide between Scotland (and Northern Ireland) on the one hand, and England (and Wales) on the other. On a turnout of 67.2%, Scotland voted 62% to stay, while on a turnout of 72.2%, the UK as a whole voted 51.9% to leave. Scotland's constitutional future remains very much up for debate.

6

THE LAW OF THE LAND

❖

Scottish law is quite distinct from English law. It is commonly said that Scots law is based upon the laws of Rome, but this is not really the case. Some concepts, however, do seem to have been taken over in their entirety from Roman law, for example the concept of *lenocinium* in which a husband connives at his wife's adultery in order to share in any material gain.

The question of exactly how Scots law developed is a matter perhaps best left in detail to the experts (the *Encyclopaedia Britannica* article on the subject is a good starting point for the really curious, or really sad), but it seems that up until the seventeenth century Scots law was a matter of Scottish common law, a core of traditions and precedents adapted and amended (as in most countries) through time.

In the seventeenth century the Scots apparently began to follow the practice of Dutch and French jurists who had built their own legal systems using Roman law, thereby 'plugging' the holes in Scots common law by applying classical precedents. By the time the Union of England and Scotland came about in 1707, the differences between the two systems were quite marked, particularly with regard to the concept of equity, where Scots law retains the original meaning of something that is fair and 'equitable'. This is not to say – as some sentimentally inclined Scots do say – that Scottish law is necessarily therefore kinder than English law, but it does mean that Scottish courts have had more discretion than English courts, and is therefore one of the ways in which Scottish law is, as the *Britannica* says, aligned alongside the 'continental civil law and not the English system'.

King James I has been credited with introducing what has been claimed to be the world's first free state aid – the 'Poor's Roll' – with an Act in 1424: 'and gif there bee onie pure [poor] creature, for faulte of cunning, or expenses, that cannot, nor may not follow his cause, the King for the love of GOD, sall ordain the judge to purwey and get a leill and a wise Advocate, to follow sik pure creatures causes.' (James had just been set free from English captivity, had a bad-tempererd relationship with the Scottish parliament, and was very likely in sympathy with the oppressed.)

After 1707, some aspects of Scottish law – particularly with regard to mercantile law – merged with English law, but the two remain separate systems, and indeed the existence of this 'national' system of law has long been pointed to by Scottish nationalists, who say that two nations with such different legal systems should not be joined at the hip in an artificial union.

The aspect of Scots law that attracts most attention in modern times is, of course, the third verdict open to Scottish courts in a criminal trial apart from 'Guilty' and 'Not Guilty' – the famous (or infamous) verdict of 'Not Proven'. The verdict of 'Not Guilty' is taken everywhere to mean (in theory at least) that the defendant leaves the court without a stain on their character, but 'Not Proven' has always carried a stigma summed up by its detractors as, 'We know ye did it but cannae prove it.'

The 'Not Proven' option made a surprise entrance into the American House of Representatives impeachment proceedings against President Bill Clinton in 1998–9. When the vote was taken, the perjury charge against the President was backed by 45 votes and rejected by 55 votes. Republican Senator Arlen Specter announced he was not convinced that Clinton had received a fair trial and invoked Scottish law, declaring his vote to be for 'Not Proven'; his choice was ordered by the Chief Justice to be recorded as 'Not Guilty'.

The legal profession in Scotland distinguishes 'advocates' from 'Solicitors'. Advocates function pretty much as barristers do in England, and are occasionally derided by those outside that select grouping as having an unwarranted tendency to regard themselves as an elite body. Solicitors have traditionally stuck to representing their clients in the lower courts, but this practice – like much else in Scottish law – is an evolving state of affairs.

——— Ten Memorable Scottish Trials ———

Scottish trials have often created significant legal precedents, or been of historical import or simply been memorable. Here are ten examples of the Scottish legal system in all its glory – and shame.

THOMAS AIKENHEAD IS TRIED AND EXECUTED FOR BLASPHEMY (1696)

An ancient Chinese curse says, 'May you live in interesting times' and the 1690s were interesting times in Scotland. William of Orange had come to the throne in 1689, and the 'divine right' of kings to rule was up for discussion, as were all systems of government; theists were quietly distinguishing themselves from Christians, deists were even more quietly distancing themselves from theists, and atheists kept completely silent – apart from a few daring oddballs such as Thomas Aikenhead. Aikenhead, a student at the University of Edinburgh, was brought before the Scottish Privy Council in 1696, charged with blasphemy, indicted, and brought to trial. He was accused of:

> having repeatedly maintained, in conversation, that theology was a rhapsody of ill-invented nonsense, patched up partly of the moral doctrines of philosophers, and partly of poetical fictions and extravagant chimera… That he called the New Testament the history of the impostor Christ; That he said Moses was the better artist and the better politician; and he preferred Mahomet to Christ; That the Holy Scriptures were stuffed with such madness, nonsense, and contradictions, that he admired the stupidity of the world in being so long deluded by them; That he rejected the mystery of the Trinity as unworthy of refutation; and scoffed at the incarnation of Christ.

He was also alleged to have said that Christianity would be gone by 1800.

Aikenhead was certainly not alone in his beliefs, and the Lord Advocate, Sir James Stewart, was determined to make an example of him, despite what seems to have been a partial (and wholly understandable) recantation of his views (though he insisted, even on the gallows, that moral laws were of human rather than divine origin). Aikenhead was found guilty and hanged – the last person to be hanged for blasphemy in Britain. The case shocked many in Britain, and in London the 'common sense' philosopher John Locke collected every report he could find of the trial (which ensured that the trial details were preserved, and that Aikenhead's name would not be forgotten). For nineteenth-century rationalists, the Scottish clergy were a notable bunch of hypocrites and villains: Thomas Babington Macaulay raged: 'the preachers who were the poor boy's murderers… insulted heaven with prayers more blasphemous than anything he had uttered.'

WITCH HUNT: JANET HORNE IS CONDEMNED TO BE BURNED ALIVE (1727)

After Cromwell finally defeated the Scots during the Civil War, his regime brought an end to the 'great Scottish witch hunt of 1649–50' – a 'Kirk Party' led reign of terror which had resulted in the execution of over 300 people, mostly lower-class women. Witchcraft was a crime in England as well, of course, and around 200 'witches' were executed in East Anglia during the brief reign of terror of the so-called 'Witchfinder General', Matthew Hopkins, but Scotland was a particularly bad country in which to be accused of witchcraft – only in Protestant parts of Scotland, however: no Catholic area (which were mainly in the Highlands) is known to have executed a witch.

Witchcraft was made a crime in Scotland in 1563 at the instigation of the Church of Scotland. When James VI of Scotland – a firm believer in witchcraft – became King of England as James I, he extended existing English laws against witchcraft with the Witchcraft Act of 1604, which brought England into line with Scotland by making it easier to convict and execute a wider range of 'witches'.

Witchcraft trials continued in Scotland after they had lapsed in England, with notable bursts occurring in the 1660s and in 1691. The last Scottish trial and execution for witchcraft took place in Dornoch, Sutherland, and is probably Scotland's most shameful trial. Janet Horne was accused by her neighbours of turning her daughter into a pony, and of getting Satan then to shoe the pony (Janet's daughter had deformed hands and feet). Janet was weak and befuddled, and it is clear that she had no idea what was going on at the trial (the judge was later reprimanded). Mother and daughter were condemned to death but the daughter escaped, one hopes with help from someone. Janet was led to the place of execution – where she is said to have warmed her hands at the fire – and burned alive in a tar barrel.

Nine years later, in 1736, the UK parliament passed the Witchcraft Act, forbidding execution for witchcraft. The response of the Church of Scotland was to protest that this consequence of the Act of Union meant that Scotland could no longer burn its own witches (as commanded by the Bible). The Associate Presbytery at Edinburgh was still fuming in 1743, declaring the Witchcraft Act to be 'contrary to the express law of God, for which a holy God may be provoked in a way of righteous judgment'.

JOSEPH KNIGHT BECOMES A FREE MAN (1777–8)

'Joseph Knight' was born in Africa around 1753, was captured and enslaved, and acquired his name when he was bought by a man called Knight, who, in about 1766, sold the boy on in Jamaica to a Scottish Jacobite planter called John Wedderburn. Scots owned and managed many of the slave plantations in Jamaica, which were a source of great wealth for Scotland. The terrible conditions under which the slaves were kept there were well known in Britain: Dr Johnson proposed a toast to the next slave rebellion in the West Indies around this time, and he was not alone in his sympathies.

When Wedderburn returned to Scotland in 1768, he took Joseph with him. Knight was baptized by a Church of Scotland minister, and – said Knight later – Wedderburn promised to free him in seven years' time, 'if he behaved well'. However, Knight formed a liaison with a servant called Anne (later ungallantly described in court as 'one of the Fair Sex not very famous for her virtues').

They had a child, who died, and the couple were married against Wedderburn's wishes in 1773; Wedderburn refused to rehire Anne or even house the pair of them. Joseph, however, was well aware of Lord Mansfield's landmark 1772 judgement in England that slavery was unlawful in England: 'Whatever inconveniences... may follow.' (The judgement had no bearing on the slave trade or on slavery in British possessions abroad.)

Joseph decided to test the law and left Wedderburn, who promptly sought a warrant from justices of the peace – which was granted – to have his slave detained (the justices in question were linked in several ways to Wedderburn and had done nicely themselves out of slavery). Joseph then managed to have the case brought before John Swinton, a sheriff-depute at Perth who was known to be against slavery. Swinton ruled that 'the State of Slavery is not recognised by the Laws of this Kingdom and is inconsistent with the principles thereof and Found that the Regulations in Jamaica concerning slaves do not extend to this Kingdom and repelled the Defender's Claim to perpetual Service.'

Wedderburn (referred to in court as 'the complainer') appealed to the court of session, where he argued that whatever may be the case with slavery 'perpetual servitude' of labour was enshrined in Scots law. Joseph's case was argued by the Lord Advocate, Henry Dundas. The court backed Swinton's ruling against slavery by eight to four, with Lord Auchinleck declaring that Joseph Knight was 'our brother; and he is a man, although not our colour' (in London, Dr Johnson told Boswell, Auchinleck's son, that he would fund Knight's case).

Significant as the trial was, Joseph Knight – and Scotland's involvement in slavery – largely disappeared from the Scottish consciousness, until the publication of James Robertson's novel *Joseph Knight* (2003).

THE DOUBLE LIFE OF DEACON BRODIE (1788)

William Brodie appeared to be the unexceptionable product of a respectable Edinburgh middle-class family. His father was a prosperous cabinetmaker, while his mother came from the minor gentry – a common merger of the day. Born in 1746, Brodie was educated at Edinburgh High School and entered the family business in 1756. It is claimed that his dark desires for a less respectable life were awoken by seeing a performance of John Gay's *The Beggar's Opera* (an early example of the perceived pernicious effect on nice middle-class children of bad cultural examples).

By 1781, Brodie had become a deacon, one of the city's leading trades representatives. It has also been claimed (with retrospective wisdom) that Brodie abused his position for his own enrichment, but the extent to which his activities in that role differed from those of any other deacon remains unclear. What is clear is that the respectable citizen was engaged in nefarious activities, organizing burglaries with a gang from Edinburgh's criminal underworld. Eventually, one of the gang turned informer, and Brodie came to trial in 1788 (he had fled to Holland, where he planned to leave for America, but was extradited).

The trial was conducted by Lord Braxfield, one of Scotland's less liberal legal figures, and Brodie's fate was sealed after the tools of his thieving trade were discovered in his house – pistols, masks, and many keys. Brodie was hanged with an accomplice on the Tollbooth gallows; popular myth insists that he designed this 'improved' gallows and that he was its first victim.

The trial's exposure of Brodie's double life, with its unsettling exposure of the dark side of respectable society, inspired Robert Louis Stevenson's *The Strange Case of Dr Jekyll and Mr Hyde* (1886).

'THE SPIRIT OF FREEDOM': THE TRIAL OF THOMAS MUIR FOR SEDITION (1793)

Born in 1765, the Scottish advocate Thomas Muir was one of many young European men and women radicalized by the revolutionary ferment following the French Revolution. Muir became a leading member of the Friends of the People Society – a group of reform-minded people mainly drawn from the middle-ranking mercantile classes, which campaigned (in a mild sort of way) for parliamentary and social reform.

The British government overreacted to such organizations, and Muir – a known republican – was arrested in 1793. Released on bail, he went to France to plead (with Tom Paine) for the moderate cause in France and against the execution of Louis XVI. He returned to Scotland and ended up in court in front of that dreaded reactionary, Scotland's own 'hanging judge', Lord Braxfield. Braxfield – who once said, 'Let them bring me prisoners, and I will find them law' – shocked everyone by sentencing Muir to fourteen years transportation to Australia. Muir was well treated on the voyage, and also well treated in Australia, as just about everyone recognized that an injustice had been done.

Muir escaped from Australia aboard an American ship bound for California, but frustratingly he never made it to the United States. He eventually died in obscurity in France, in 1799. An imposing 90-foot obelisk to Muir's memory was erected in Edinburgh's Waterloo Place in 1845.

The great Scottish jurist Lord Cockburn described the case as one of 'the cases the memory whereof never perisheth. History cannot let its injustice alone.' As for the appalling Braxfield, he is the model for Lord Weir in Stevenson's unfinished novel, *Weir of Hermiston*. Cockburn described Braxfield as 'like a formidable blacksmith. His accent and his dialect were exaggerated Scotch; his language, like his thoughts, short, strong, and conclusive.' However, Muir was also strong and conclusive, and it is his words from an Edinburgh prison that still resonate: 'The spirit of freedom is not extinguished, but still remains its formal energy, in defiance of the artifices and the violence of despotism.'

WILLIAM HARE TESTIFIES AGAINST WILLIAM BURKE (1828)

The Burke and Hare murders occurred in Edinburgh in 1827–8 and the case remains one of the most famous in criminal history. By the late 1820s, demand in Scotland from the medical profession for cadavers for dissection had reached an all-time high; so high that bodies were being stolen both on spec and to order by specialist grave-robbers – 'body snatchers' or 'resurrection men' – for selling on to the medical profession.

William Burke and William Hare may have met earlier, but their professional relationship began when Burke moved (with his partner and accomplice Helen MacDougal) into a lodging house run by Hare and his wife Margaret (also an accomplice). According to Hare's later testimony their first sale was in 1827, to the Edinburgh Medical College, of one of Hare's freshly dead (of natural causes) lodgers. This was when they first met the man who was to be the 'demand' side of their business – the respected anatomist Professor Robert Knox. The next cadaver was that of a sickly tenant called Joseph the Miller, whose death they hastened by rendering him incapable with whisky and then suffocating him, a process they found to be both simple and effective.

Burke and Hare's victims, drawn from Edinburgh's impoverished underclass, possibly totalled seventeen. The fresher the corpse, the more money they got. They favoured prostitutes as victims, and one was recognized on the dissecting table by some of the students. Another victim, 'Daft Jamie', was a well-known character about town.

The pair were eventually arrested after one of Hare's lodgers discovered a body hidden under a bed, but the evidence against the pair was circumstantial and not strong. The Lord Advocate offered Hare a deal: his freedom (and that of the women) for conclusive evidence against Burke. Hare agreed, and Burke was condemned to death at the Edinburgh High Court on Christmas Eve 1828. Huge crowds had gathered outside to hear the verdict, and an even larger crowd – perhaps 40,000 people – gathered to watch Burke's execution. An observer noted: 'It is usual after an execution, for the people to hurry away as if half ashamed of being there, or as if they were glad to get off – a feeling of relief, a sort of queer, strange feeling of terror. Not so here; but a feeling of Sweet revenge or justice seemed to have taken possession of the onlookers.'

Burke's body was given up for dissection: a large crowd of non-anatomy students tried to get in and a near riot broke out: as was noted, 'a regular melee took place in which some of the police were worsted, and used their batons freely'. Some of Burke's skin was allegedly used to bind a book which can be seen (if you are that morbid) in the Surgeons' Hall Museum in Edinburgh.

The Burke and Hare murders led to the Anatomy Act of 1832, in which the supply of cadavers to medical schools was regulated. Hare and the two women made themselves scarce. For many people, then and now, the real villain of the affair was the sinister Robert Knox, who was forced to resign, but went on to make a good living out of writing and lecturing.

THE CASE OF THE DEADLY COCOA: DID MADELEINE KILL HER LOVER? (1857)

Madeleine Smith, born in 1835, was a young upper-class woman living a life of respectable conformity in 1850s Glasgow; Emile L'Angelier was a Jerseyman of French origin, who was working as a clerk in Glasgow. The two struck up a friendship, and became secretly engaged in 1855. Madeleine's passion cooled, however (her parents had found a nice rich young man for her) and she tried to break off the relationship; Emile got upset and threatened to send her love letters to her father. Madeleine then bought some arsenic at an apothecary's shop, which she signed for, saying it was needed to kill rats. She bought arsenic twice more over the next few weeks, giving the same reason. Emile subsequently died of arsenic poisoning (you can buy a poster of a Victorian artist's impression of the stricken Emile online, should you wish), and Madeleine was arrested for his murder. The prosecution alleged that Madeleine had given Emile cocoa laced with arsenic (an image that sent chills down the back of many a lover and/or husband). Madeleine was not allowed to speak in court; her defence suggested that Emile had either killed himself or had been taking the arsenic as a tonic and overdosed.

The case, quickly dubbed 'The Trial of the Century', gripped Scotland, indeed Britain: illicit sex, class barriers overthrown, murder – classic *News of the World* stuff (the *NoW* was founded in 1843), and, to cap everything, the Scottish court returned the classic 'Not Proven' verdict. Madeleine moved to London and was married in 1861, and details of her life thereafter are tantalizingly sketchy; she may have became a socialist, and moved to New York, where, says the *Dictionary of National Biography*, she was threatened with deportation as an undesirable alien at the age of ninety. She died in 1928, and remains a much pondered figure, the subject of several books and novels.

The Snail in the Ginger Beer: Donoghue v. Stevenson (1932)

In 1929 a lady called Mrs Donoghue was having ice cream and a bottle of Stevenson's Ginger Beer in the Wellmeadow Café in Paisley. She had drunk some of the ginger beer and when she tipped up the rest of the bottle (which was opaque), out slithered the decomposing remains of a snail. Understandably horrified, she decided someone had to be sued, and as the owner of the shop was a nice man, she opted instead to sue the manufacturer, a local man. The case went all the way to the House of Lords, which ruled that it was indeed the manufacturer's fault.

Mrs Donoghue's case rested on the specifically Scottish concept of 'delict', a broader concept of a wrong requiring reparation than generally available under the English legal conception of 'tort' (or so lawyers say, and who can argue?). The House of Lords decided Mrs Donoghue had been caused harm and the manufacturer was to blame; she won her case, and the precedent of negligence was to be applied all over the world, as consumers (and their lawyers) became aware of their rights.

All fizzy drinks in the west of Scotland are dubbed 'ginger' by the natives, and it is sometimes claimed that the drink in question may not actually have been ginger beer, but it seems fairly clear it was.

'TURN UP THE RADIO AND I'LL GO QUIETLY': PETER MANUEL (1958)

Scotland's most notorious serial killer, Peter Manuel, was born in New York in 1927 to Scottish parents. The family moved to Coventry in 1932, and he received his first conviction, for a sexual assault, aged sixteen. After serving time in jail for rape, Manuel moved to Glasgow to be with his family in 1953.

Manuel's first known killing, one of several he later confessed to, was of a seventeen-year-old girl in 1956. Manuel's murders were brutal, rapid in conception and execution, and seem to have been utterly random.

Manuel was finally brought to trial in 1958 and charged with the murder of seven people. He electrified all of Scotland by opting to conduct his own defence at the Glasgow High Court, but failed to convince the judge, Lord Cameron, that he was a medical rather than a criminal case: Cameron later wrote: 'I saw no sign indicative to a layman of any illness or abnormality beyond callousness, selfishness and treachery in high degree, but I did form the impression that he was even then laying the foundation of a suggestion that he might in the end of the day be presented not as a criminal, but as one in need of medical care.'

Manuel was found guilty of the seven murders, but detectives who worked on the Manuel case were convinced that he had murdered many more, perhaps fifteen. After shooting dead a husband and wife and their young son in Uddingston on New Year's Day 1958, he left the house, then returned to eat the family's leftover food and feed the cat; afterwards he gave a lift to a policeman in the family car. The policeman was at that time involved in searching for another of Manuel's victims, a young girl. Later, Manuel led the police to the girl's grave, saying, 'This is the place. In fact, I think I'm standing on her now.'

Manuel's calmness at his trial, his utter indifference not just to the fate of his victims, but to his own fate, shocked the nation. Led to the gallows, his last words were, 'Turn up the radio and I'll go quietly.' Brian Cox based his characterization of Hannibal Lecter in the movie *Manhunter* (1986) on Manuel.

The 'Lockerbie Bomber' case: HM Advocate v. Megrahi (2000)

In 2001 Libyan Abdelbaset Ali Mohmed al-Megrahi was convicted of causing the explosion of a Pan Am jumbo jet above the town of Lockerbie in December 1988, killing all 259 people on board and 11 in the town itself. The trial was described as a 'normal' criminal trial under Scots law, but was held without a jury in a specially designated court in the Netherlands.

Both the trial and the later dismissal of an appeal remain highly controversial, with one UN observer describing the appeal's dismissal as a 'spectacular miscarriage of justice'.

In June 2007 Prime Minister Tony Blair signed a 'memorandum of understanding' with Libya regarding prisoner exchange, which the government insisted did not cover the Lockerbie case. The 'memorandum', however, was felt by many in Scotland to be a constitutional breach, as law is a devolved matter. Scots Tory leader, Annabel Goldie, said that the UK government had 'ridden roughshod over devolution and treated with contempt Scotland's distinct and independent legal system'. On August 20 2009, Megrahi was given 'compassionate release' by order of the Scottish government. He was flown home to Libya that day.

Megrahi died in 2012. In 2016, the former Justice Secretary Kenny MacAskill published his account of the Megrahi trail – *The Lockerbie Bombing: The Search for Justice* – which received a mixed reception.

7

THE FIGHTING SCOTS

❖

'Man, am I no' a bonnie fechter?' says Alan Breck to David Balfour, shortly after joyously despatching another adversary in *Kidnapped*. Scotland has produced many such 'bonnie fechters', men (and occasionally women) for whom fighting was a trade, often a pastime, and Scots have taken up the martial trade both at home and abroad with enthusiasm.

Such traditions were endemic in both the Borders and Highlands in particular. Ever since Roman times, the area surrounding Hadrian's Wall was seen as bandit country, and up until the seventeenth century the Border marches were one of the most dangerous areas in Europe. The men who fought here rode as cavalry or marched on foot, and knew how to lay siege and hold out against siege. They knew how to steal, and how to destroy. Borderers fought their neighbours, and fought the English; those who were transplanted to Ulster fought the Irish, and then in their thousands travelled to America in the eighteenth century where they fought the Indians and the English (again) and, of course, each other. Benjamin Franklin called the Ulster Scots 'Christian white savages'.

Violence was also a way of life in the Highlands, whether in the mountains, or in the isles. Clan feuding here was often a matter of struggle over limited resources, and such fighting could be cruel and remorseless.

Scots who learned their trade at home often sold their services abroad, as mercenaries. Tens of thousands of Scots served in the brutal fighting of the Thirty Years War (1618–48). A contemporary engraving in the British Museum depicts some of these Scottish troops (three in kilts), and the text accompanying the picture says that these hardy soldiers contented themselves with 'roots and carrots' when no bread was available.

Whatever banners they fought under in Europe, these troops often had their own St Andrews flags with them, as several of the following bonnie fechters did, though not the first (who may have fought under a raven banner).

—— Ten Bonnie Fechters ——

SWEYN ASLEIFFSON (c.1115–c.1171)

Regarded by many as the last and 'greatest' of all the Vikings, Asleiffson was born in Caithness. His father was Olaf, lord of the Norwegian lands of Orkney and Caithness, and Sweyn's long and bloody career is documented in the *Orkneyinga Saga* (written or compiled later in Iceland, the saga details the fighting lives of the Earls of Orkney). Outlawed in his youth for a casual killing, Sweyn went into exile in the Hebrides, where he grew to be a talented player in the complex and merciless world of Norse/Scottish dynastic struggle. Around 1139, Sweyn succeeded his father and raided and feuded for some thirty years, his depredations reaching down to the Scilly Isles. The sagamen say he died in 1171 while attacking Dublin. The Irish and Anglo-Norman sources say this particular Orcadian attack was led by a Viking called 'John the Mad' (or 'John the Very Angry'), which description may or may not refer to Sweyn. His implausible dying 'confession' in the *Orkneyinga Saga* is generally regarded as a pious invention, but like many Viking lords of this period the appalling Sweyn was probably just as content to found a church as a drinking hall – or to burn either, if they weren't his.

WILLIAM ARMSTRONG, 'KINMONT WILLIE' (fl.1569–1603)

Kinmont Willie is regarded as one of the more fearsome of the Border reivers, which means he was a serious hard case indeed. A descendant of the aptly named 'Ill Will' Armstrong, Willie took an oath to obey the monarch and wardens in 1569, and may even have kept it for a few weeks before resuming raiding; in the summer he led 400 Armstrongs across the border. Like all the Border chiefs, Willie was an equal-opportunity plunderer and raided against the Scots as well as the English, while taking care not to attack English Armstrongs and other allies; indeed, the Scottish Armstrongs (like the Maxwells), often allied themselves with England.

Willie's fearful talents were frequently employed by his betters, not just on the border but further north. In 1585, as part of an 'official' expedition, his forces ravaged the city of Stirling, stealing the very bars from the windows. When Armstrong was seized and imprisoned in Carlisle Castle during a truce in 1596, there were cries of 'foul' from the Scots as – in theory at least – truces were sacrosanct. His sensational escape (which annoyed Elizabeth I) is described in one of the great Border ballads, 'Kinmont Willie'.

> 'Farewell, farewell, my gude Lord Scroope!
> My gude Lord Scroope, farewell!' he cried;
> 'I'll pay you for my lodging-maill,
> When first we meet on the border-side.'

In 1596 it was rumoured that James VI was considering turning Willie loose on the citizens of Edinburgh following a riot. His end is not recorded, but he is said to have died peacefully in bed.

Patrick Ferguson (1744–80)

Patrick Ferguson was very much a product of the Scottish Enlightenment. The family lived on Edinburgh's High Street, and knew everybody who mattered.

Ferguson joined the Scots Greys, fought in the Seven Years War, and invented a weapon of mass destruction: the world's first breech-loading rifle (the army later refused to adopt Ferguson's rifle, labelling it 'barbarous'). In 1777, during the American War of Independence, Ferguson and three of his riflemen – all armed with prototypes of his new weapon – were spying on the American lines by a creek called the Brandywine in Pennsylvania, when two horsemen appeared, an officer and his aide; Ferguson and his men could each get off four rounds a minute, and could certainly have killed the officer, but Ferguson – ever the gentleman – thought it 'not pleasant to fire at the back of an unoffending individual who was acquitting himself cooly of his duty, and so I let him alone'. Rather quaintly, he instead rose from cover and asked the men to surrender: the startled horsemen rode back to their lines. Ferguson was wounded in the following Battle of the Brandywine, and was told that he had spared George Washington's life; he had no regrets.

Ferguson was later killed at the Battle of Kings Mountain, where he was the only known non-American combatant. His body was stripped and then urinated on by the Patriot Militia. In 1930 the Americans erected a fine headstone over the grave of the gallant Ferguson, who is buried beside his female companion, a 'buxom redhead' called Virginia Sal, who was also killed by the Patriots. Sal is not mentioned on the head-stone, sadly.

JOHN PAUL JONES (1747–92)
Jones was born 'John Paul' in a cottage, the son of a Kirkcud-bright gardener. He went to sea aged thirteen in a merchant ship, and, like many sailors of his day, served on board slave-ships. The Atlantic merchant trade was a hard one, and after he became a captain (in 1768) he gained a reputation as a noted flogger and his crews were often mutinous. He once killed a mutineer, and was accused of killing a boy by flog-ging him into permanent ill health. Like many a merchant in difficulty, he joined the freemasons for protection and moved to America, where he eventually became known as John Paul Jones. He became captain of an American sloop in 1775 and rapidly acquired a name as a first-rate warship captain. He destroyed and also captured many British ships, prizes that not only hindered the British war effort but added wealth and confidence to the cause. He took the war to the British coast, launched a raid on Whitehaven, and threatened the port of Leith with bombardment unless he was bought off (the wind blew his ship back out to sea).

At Catherine the Great's request, he became a Russian admi-ral, and commanded a Russian fleet in fierce action against the Turks. He is regarded as the founder of the American navy, and is buried in the US Naval Academy chapel.

SIR JOHN MOORE (1761–1809)
After attending Glasgow High School, Moore somehow man-aged to enlist as an ensign in the 51st Foot at the tender age of fourteen. While serving in America, he was almost captured

in 1779 in a sudden attack by rebels; he was 'develishly' frightened, said the young soldier, now a teenage captain. Moore became MP for Linlithgow in 1784, but never spoke in parliament; he resigned in 1790 after assuming command, as lieutenant-colonel, of his old regiment.

In 1794 Moore was ordered to Corsica to aid the anti-French resistance, where he proved to be a cautious and successful commander. Like Sir Colin Campbell (see below), Moore was unwilling to risk his men's lives for no good reason. In the decisive attack on the citadel of Calvi, being bombarded by young Captain Nelson, he commanded an assault force of grenadiers. Nelson (who was somewhat sniffy about his rival hero) lost an eye in the battle, and Moore took a shell splinter in the head. Moore wrote to his mother: 'You have heard how the thickness of my skull saved my life. The last plaster fell off to-day; and as soon as the hair, which has been shaved, grows, there will not remain any trace of the hurt.'

The head wound was the first of several wounds in a life of many campaigns: in 1801, near Alexandria, his horse was killed beneath him and he almost lost his leg. His luck ran out during the Peninsular War, when he was struck by cannon shot at Corunna. His last words were, 'Stanhope, remember me to your sister' (the sister in question was that remarkable traveller, Lady Hester Stanhope; she kept Moore's bloodstained glove for the rest of her life). Moore's burial inspired what was once one of the most popular poems in the English language, Charles Wolfe's 'The Burial of Sir John Moore after Corunna'.

> Not a drum was heard, not a funeral note,
> As his corse to the rampart we hurried;
> Not a soldier discharged his farewell shot
> O'er the grave where our hero we buried.

THOMAS COCHRANE, 10TH EARL OF DUNDONALD
(1775–1860)

Thomas Cochrane belongs to a select group of people indeed: not only did he become a national hero for two nations, he was also the model for a great fictional hero, Patrick O'Brian's Jack Aubrey. Cochrane joined his first ship at the age of seventeen, and early on displayed the qualities of the Royal Navy's 'fighting captains': decisiveness, bravery and a sound knowledge of his ships and men. Cochrane's fellow captains came from all backgrounds and, as Jane Austen fans know, were the heroes of the age. And Cochrane was the best. He fought the Spanish, the French (missed out on the Americans), pirates, and privateers. He became an MP, but – like many sea-dogs – was completely out of his depth, and ended up embroiled in intrigue. In 1817 he was invited by the Chilean government to organize their navy. Cochrane threw himself into the South American wars of liberation with gusto, and Pablo Neruda wrote a collection of poems, *Lord Cochrane de Chile* (1970), in tribute to him. He was buried in Westminster Abbey, mourned by many throughout the world.

SIR COLIN CAMPBELL, BARON CLYDE (1792–1863)

Born in Glasgow as Colin Macliver, Campbell was the son of a carpenter whose wife was the sister of Colonel Campbell of Islay. The colonel bought the young man a commission (under the name of Campbell) in 1807, and Ensign Campbell served with distinction in the Peninsular War (1808–13). His bravery (he was wounded several times) led to him being awarded a company in 1813. He went on to serve in Britain's imperial wars in India and China. In 1854, at the Battle of Balaclava during the Crimean War, his outnumbered 93rd Highlanders held the line against a charge by Russian cavalry: 'Damn all that eagerness!' he shouted, as some of his men advanced out of line.

The action was witnessed by war correspondent William Russell of *The Times*, who described the Highlanders as 'that thin red streak tipped with a line of steel', a description modified in popular culture as 'the thin red line'. The Indian mutiny broke out in 1856, and Campbell, now commander-in-chief of the army, raised the siege of Lucknow with his force of Sikhs and Highlanders. Campbell's pipers also entered popular culture, with many paintings and (later, of course) movies depicting weary defenders hearing the distant bagpipes of Campbell's men. Campbell was described as 'Old Slowcoach' because of his cautious approach to campaigning – but he rarely lost an action once committed, and has been credited with saving the British Empire in India.

SIR HECTOR MACDONALD (1853–1903)

The son of a poor Highland crofter, Macdonald enlisted as a private in the Gordon Highlanders, and rose through the ranks while serving in India, becoming a young colour sergeant in 1874. He saw active service in the second Anglo-Afghan War, and in 1880 his bravery led to his commission as a second lieutenant. In South Africa, during the Anglo–Transvaal War, he was taken prisoner after the Battle of Majuba Hill, but his sword was returned to him by General Joubert in recognition of his 'conspicuous gallantry'. In the Egyptian campaigns, he commanded a (mainly Sudanese) brigade at the Battle of Omdurman in 1898, where his fast reactions prevented the exposed British flank being turned – the decisive action of the battle. Now known as 'Fighting Mac', he became a brigadier-general in 1899. After service against the Boers, he was given command of the British forces in Ceylon, where he became embroiled in the bitter colonial politics, and was accused of seducing boys. He returned to Britain where he was ordered to go back to Ceylon to clear his name. Macdonald set off for Ceylon, but shot himself in a Paris hotel room. His death sparked what the *Dictionary of National Biography* calls 'massive public grief in Scotland'. He was buried at Dean Cemetery in Edinburgh, where tens of thousands came to mourn the great soldier (his tomb is splendid). Some years after his death, a bizarre rumour spread: he had not really died, and people said he was serving under an assumed name in foreign armies; the German General von Mackensen was a favourite candidate for his new incarnation.

SIMON FRASER, 15TH LORD LOVAT (1911–95)

The 15th Lord Lovat, and 25th chief of Clan Fraser, was a direct descendant of the villainous 11th Lord Lovat but was a much finer man. A product of the Roman Catholic aristocracy, Lovat joined the regiment raised by his father, the Lovat Scouts, on the outbreak of the Second World War in 1939 (three of his uncles had died in the First World War). He became a commando leader in 1941, in which year he captured an Enigma code machine in a Norway raid – pausing at the local post office to send a cheeky telegram to Hitler (who put a bounty on his head). In 1942, during the otherwise disastrous Dieppe raid, Lovat, armed with a Winchester rifle, and his men destroyed a German battery, preventing greater casualties. On D-Day in 1944 Lovat, accompanied by his piper, led the British commandos ashore on Sword Beach and fought his way inland to Pegasus Bridge. A third of his brigade were casualties, and Lovat himself was badly wounded. Churchill sent Lovat to Moscow as an emissary, observing to Stalin that Lovat was 'the mildest-mannered man that ever scuttled a ship or cut a throat'.

SIR DAVID STIRLING (1915–90)

A member of Scotland's Roman Catholic aristocracy (his wife was one of the Lovats), Stirling's childhood ambition of climbing Everest was cut short by the Second World War. He trained as a commando officer, and in 1942 formed a unit for fighting behind German lines in North Africa. Stirling's new force – the Special Air Service – distinguished itself throughout the remainder of the war. Taken prisoner in 1943, Stirling made four escape attempts before being incarcerated in high-security Colditz. The SAS was disbanded at the end of the war, but was later re-formed (with Stirling's involvement) and is now one of the most highly regarded elite fighting forces in the world.

—— Ten Bloody Battles ——

Scots love their bloody battles. The next best thing to gloating over a defeat of the English (e.g. Bannockburn) is sobbing over a defeat by the English (e.g. Flodden). Freudians call this sadomasochism; Scots call it patriotism. Although tempted, I have stuck here to describing battles that actually happened, as opposed to battles that may or may not have happened, such as the supposed Battle of Athelstaneford *c*.AD 832, when a combined force of Picts and Scots is said to have defeated an English army after St Andrew placed his white cross in the blue sky to encourage the Scots/Picts to victory. After the battle, either the Scots or the Picts got to take home King Athelstane's head ('ma ba'). Subsequently the Scots – and maybe also the Picts – adopted the Saltire as their flag.

MONS GRAUPIUS (C.AD 83)
This battle between the Caledonians and the Romans is known to us solely from the testimony of Roman historian Tacitus, who was writing some years after the event. Tacitus was, however, the son-in-law of Agricola, the general who won the battle, and his overall account is regarded as reliable. The

site of Mons Graupius is uncertain: probably somewhere in the foothills of the Grampians. The speech given by the Caledonian leader Calgacus to his warriors on the eve of the battle is one of the most famous in antiquity: Calgacus tells his men the Romans 'make a desert, and call it peace'. (The speech may well, however, be a complete invention by Tacitus, and simply an example of Roman moralizing.) The battle resulted in a stunning victory for the Romans, who may have used only their auxiliaries in battle, keeping the legions in reserve. Tacitus gives the Caledonian death toll as around 10,000 with Roman losses a precise 360.

DUNNICHEN OR NECHTANSMERE (685)
Pictish raiders had been raiding the south lands ever since the collapse of Roman power in Britain, and in 685 Ecgfrith, King of Anglo-Saxon Northumbria, hit back at the north with a strike force and engaged the Picts (who were led by their king Bridei III) in Inverness-shire. The Northumbrian warriors were led into a swamp and hacked to pieces, with Ecgfrith among the dead. The Pictish victory was a decisive one, and discouraged further Northumbrian incursions – or, more accurately, reprisal raids – into Pictish lands. The magnificent Pictish symbol stone in Aberlemno churchyard, the Kailyard Stone, has a battle scene incised on it which has traditionally been held to represent the battle, a belief that is now generally accepted.

LARGS (1263)
The Scottish–Norwegian War of 1262–6 was fought over ownership of the Hebrides. An invading Norwegian force led by Haakon IV of Norway was stranded by foul weather at Largs, but Haakon's force of around 800 men fought off an attack by a much larger Scottish force led by King Alexander

III; the Norwegians may have been outnumbered ten to one, but managed to hold off the Scots and refloat their longships. The result of the battle itself is generally described as 'inconclusive', but a Norwegian victory would have had enormous consequences for the history of Scotland. The Scots gained sovereignty over the Hebrides in 1265. There is a pleasing legend that the Norwegians were on a surprise raid but alerted the Scots by howling in pain after stepping on thistles – this possibly led to the adoption of the thistle as Scotland's national symbol. One of Haakon's warriors bore the splendid name of Ogmund Crouchdance, but there is no evidence he got it from stepping on thistles.

STIRLING BRIDGE (1297)

This battle of the Scottish Wars of Independence is familiar to most people from Mel Gibson's movie *Braveheart* (1995), but pretty much all the movie has in common with the real battle is that the Scots won (Gibson left out the bridge, for a start). The English were led, as they often were down the centuries, by an Earl of Surrey, but – luckily for Scotland – this one was not as canny a tactician as most Earls of Surrey were. Disastrously over-confident, Surrey led his men (many of his troops were in fact Welsh) across a narrow bridge towards the Scots. The Scots leaders, Moray and Wallace (the latter, as it happens, may have been of Strathclyde Briton descent), sent their men forward, and split the English force in two. The River Forth became clogged with English soldiers trying to flee, and the Scots began a killing spree, spearing and hamstringing the packed, screaming horses to get at the riders. A group of knights, led by Sir Marmaduke Tweng, heroically cut their way back across the bridge, which Surrey then had burned, abandoning his troops. Over 5,000 of the English and Welsh died, either on the field or cut down while fleeing. The body of Hugh de Cressingham, Edward's treasurer in Scotland, was skinned, and pieces were handed out as trophies to the Scots leaders – Wallace is said to have had a baldrick made out of his bit.

After the battle, Wallace led an army into the north of England and left a swathe of desolation behind him, burning hundreds of helpless villages. The Lanercost chronicle accuses the Scots of 'burnings, depredations and murders', and though there is evidence that Wallace was angered by the desecrations of church property by his troops, there is little doubt that civilians suffered badly. The following year, Edward I led an army north and routed Wallace's forces at the Battle of Falkirk.

BANNOCKBURN (1314)

Bannockburn is regarded by many as the most important battle in Scottish history. The invading English army was led by Edward II, the Scots by Robert the Bruce. The English were possibly better equipped and certainly outnumbered the Scots at least two to one. On the morale front, however, the Scots were for once more or less united – although Bruce had many Scottish enemies riding with Edward, for a change he had few enemies at his back – while Edward's relationship with his nobles was pretty fractious. The struggle was a hard one. On the first day Bruce slew the great warrior Sir Henry de Bohun with one blow of his axe, splitting the knight's helmet and skull in two. Inspired by Bruce's heroics, the Scottish spearmen, manoeuvring with speed, shattered the charges of the heavily armoured English cavalry. By the close of day, the field was strewn with the English dead. The second day of battle began as bloodily, and under pressure Edward's army broke and fled back across the Bannock Burn. Edward himself had to be forcibly removed by his men from the battle. Scottish independence was formally acknowledged by England ten years later.

OTTERBURN (1388)

This was one of the major medieval England versus Scotland matches. The Scots were led by Earl Douglas and the English by the great (but as impetuous as Shakespeare depicts him) Hotspur. The turning point in the engagement came in the moonlight when Douglas's men charged the English calling, 'A Douglas! A Douglas!' Douglas himself was killed, but the English were defeated with heavy losses. English reinforcements (led by the Bishop of Durham) turned back when they encountered the fleeing English troops. Douglas is popularly supposed to have had a premonition of his death, as eerily recounted in the 'Ballad of Otterburn':

> Last night I dreamed a dreary dream
> Beyond the Isle of Skye;
> I dreamed that I had killed a man
> And I dreamed that man was I.

FLODDEN (1513)

Flodden was the second bloodiest battle fought on British soil (after Towton Heath) and involved the largest numbers of combatants in an England–Scotland battle. The Scots under James IV had invaded England with an army of around 30,000 men, and occupied the high ground on Flodden Hill to await an attack by the English, an army of 27,000 men led by the Earl of Surrey.

Surrey, however, simply swung his army behind the Scots, and cut off retreat to Scotland. James was thus forced to abandon his position and give battle. The Scots advanced with their dreaded 18-foot pikes and drove the English back. The English cavalry swept in, the pike formations broke up, and the English begin to mince the Scots, who were taking heavy casualties from the English billmen and longbowmen. While both sides had artillery, the English field pieces were not just lighter to move, but also more powerful, and more effective. James was killed fighting to the death, along with many of his nobles; over 9,000 Scots died that day (English losses were around 1,500). Flodden was Scotland's greatest military disaster.

SOLWAY MOSS (1542)

In a time of frequent raid and counter-raid, King James V sent a huge army of perhaps as many as 18,000 men under Lord Maxwell towards England. This formidable army was met at Solway Moss by a much smaller English force of 3,000 men led by that canny Border lord Sir Thomas Wharton. The outcome should have been an easy victory for the Scots; but the Scots leaders fell out over tactics, and Wharton, a man familiar with Border warfare, sent his 'prickers' – reiver horsemen skilled in the arts of skirmishing – against the Scots. The reivers wheeled and charged and harried, and the Scots fell apart at the seams. The battle was a complete rout, with well over 1,000 Scots being taken prisoner; whole batches surrendered to single English riders. James V died a couple of weeks later (of humiliation, it was said, but the cause was probably cholera). He was succeeded as monarch by his six-day-old daughter Mary, Queen of Scots.

THE BATTLE OF THE SHIRTS or FIELD OF SHIRTS (1544)

The Battle of the Shirts occurred during a struggle for succession to the chieftainship of the powerful Clan Ranald, and was fought beside Loch Lochy between the Frasers, led by Simon Fraser, and a powerful alliance of the Ranald, Cameron and Donald clans, led by John of Moidart. In the movies, Highland clan battles are portrayed as wild affairs with bearded half-naked men waving claymores, shouting a lot and fighting to the death. The Battle of the Shirts was pretty much like that, apart from the half-nakedness. Highlanders at this period fought wearing chain mail (if they could afford it) and this was a close-quarters engagement involving axes and the great Highland broadswords. The Frasers, hundreds of them, were killed with no quarter given. The Bishop of Ross, John Lesley, reported that no one bearing the name Fraser was left alive, and the loch was red with the blood of the slain.

CULLODEN (1746)

The last battle fought on British soil, Culloden has often been misinterpreted as an England–Scotland match. Although the Jacobite army (led by Bonnie Prince Charlie) was mainly Highland there were in fact Highland and Lowland troops on the Hanoverian side also (led by the Duke of Cumberland). Throughout England, there were Tories who wished for a Jacobite victory, while many more Scottish Protestants feared that outcome. And many in the Highland clans were just biding their time. The Jacobite forces were exhausted and ill-prepared; the government troops were fit and rested. They had a drill to repel the Highland charge, and artillery. The redcoats also believed that the Jacobites had been ordered to give no quarter. The outcome was inevitable and brutal. Pounded by artillery and volleys of musket fire, few Highlanders reached the opposite lines. Cumberland lost just over 50 men, the Jacobites over 1,000, many of them slain as they lay wounded. The artist David Morier used Jacobite prisoners as models for his painting of the battle. James Wolfe fought at Culloden and his evolving views on Highland troops mirrored those of British society (see p. 239).

There is a large modern painting in an arts centre in Portree, on the isle of Skye, depicting the horrors of the aftermath of the 1745 Rebellion, with redcoated British government troops doing terrible things to the Highlanders, killing and driving them out of their homes.

The atrocities were real enough, but if you step back outside the arts centre and look across to Skye's smaller neighbour Raasay, you are looking at the site of some of the worst horrors of the aftermath. And the horrors were perpetrated by forces under the command of two Scots, Captain Ferguson of Inverurie and Captain Scott. Ferguson's brutality is well documented, and when Flora MacDonald was given into his custody, General Campbell insisted that she 'be used with the utmost respect'. Scott was as loathsome, a disgrace to the British army. His men raped a blind girl on the island of Rona. Raasay also suffered at the hands of the MacLeod militia of Skye. The MacLeods of Raasay had been 'out' for Charlie during the '45, while the Skye MacLeods stayed at home and, like many other clanspeople, watched the Jacobite project unwind – with beady eyes fixed on the opportunity for plunder.

The Skye MacLeods stripped the island of Raasay bare, leaving the Raasay MacLeods to starve. The stark truth is that some Scottish atrocities are marketable, others are not, and in Scotland the most marketable atrocities (particularly with Americans in mind) envision redcoats driving ethereal Enya-like figures off their 'wee bit hill and glen'. The bleak ancient rule of Scottish clan feuding – watch for your neighbour's weakness and exploit it – is harder to sell to tourists.

The Eigg Massacre (1577)

Highland clan feuding may have been especially prevalent in the sixteenth-century Western Isles. Slavers and pirates could descend at any time, resources were scarce and fought over, and retribution swiftly followed any slight. The MacDonalds of Eigg had captured, bound and cast adrift some visiting MacLeods who had paid too much attention to the MacDonald women (some have seen this as a romantic affair – attempted rape is likelier). A detachment of MacLeods soon arrived seeking vengeance, but failed to find the MacDonalds who had hidden in a cave. Unfortunately, one of the MacDonalds came out of the cave to watch the departure of the MacLeods and was spotted. The MacLeods followed his tracks in the snow back to the cave, and lit a fire at the cave mouth, suffocating everyone inside – around 400 men, women, and children. Only one Eigg family – hidden in another cave – survived.

The Trumpan Massacre (1578)

The old Trumpan church on Skye is a very romantic-looking ruin, but is a place with a fearful history. The year after the Eigg massacre, a group of MacDonald warriors from Uist landed on Skye seeking revenge on the MacLeods. Finding Trumpan church full of worshippers, the MacDonalds barricaded the building and set fire to it, killing everyone inside except one badly wounded girl who escaped and raised the alarm. The MacLeods arrived in force and slew the MacDonalds, whose bodies were then buried in a dyke; this became known as the Battle of the Spoiled Dyke.

The Massacre of the Maxwells (1593)

The sixteenth-century Maxwell–Johnstone Border feud was one of the longest, bitterest, and bloodiest family feuds in British history. The Maxwells were the strongest power in the

Scottish West March, with the Johnstones not far behind. Both families raided anyone weaker than themselves (yet also provided several march wardens). The feuding between the two families somehow passed over from 'normal' predation into lasting hatred, and for decades Maxwells and Johnstones raided and killed each other. The feud reached its terrible high point on Dryfe Sands, by Lockerbie, when the Johnstones lured a force of 2,000 Maxwells, led by Lord Maxwell, into an ambush: in the ensuing slaughter, Lord Maxwell tried to surrender but was cut down, as were over 700 of his followers. The downward sword stroke used to slaughter the dismounted Maxwells became known as the 'Lockerbie Lick'.

A reconciliation was tried in 1608, between the next Lord Maxwell and the Johnstone leader: Maxwell shot Johnstone in the back (twice), for which action his lordship was later executed. The long feud then died down, almost as quickly as it arose.

THE GENTLEMAN ADVENTURERS OF FIFE
(1598–1609)

One of the oddest (and little known) episodes of Scottish history involved the splendidly named 'Gentleman Adventurers of Fife', a group of twelve lowland gentry who were granted the forfeited MacLeod lands on Lewis by James VI. All they had to do was go and take it. The king's intention was to bring the Gaelic Western Isles into line with lowland Scotland, and the colonists were given a free hand to deploy whatever measure they saw fit.

The colonists landed on Lewis in 1598 with 500 mercenaries, and over the next few years a series of bloody fights took place on both land and sea, as the MacLeods fought back, burning the Stornoway settlement. One of the MacLeod leaders was captured, and hung, drawn, and quartered at St Andrew's.

Eventually (though aided by betrayal in the MacLeod ranks), the Adventurers gave up and sold their rights to Colin Mackenzie, 1st Earl of Seaforth, in 1609. The Crown granted the Mackenzies the right to impose 'slauchter, mutilation, fyre-raising, or utheris inconvenieties'. A Mackenzie force, 700 strong, led by 'Roderick the Tutor', put Lewis to fire and sword. Lewis was part of civilized Scotland at last.

Lewis stayed in Mackenzie hands until 1844, when it was sold to a later exemplar of civilized Scotland, the opium trader Sir James Matheson.

SCOTLAND AND THE THIRTY YEARS WAR (1618–48)

The long and bloody wars that made up the Thirty Years War devastated much of Central Europe – the final casualty toll was around 8 million. Scotland's involvement in the wars is little known in popular culture, yet Scots were important players in the carnage.

Scotland was dynastically involved. Princess Elizabeth of Bohemia was the daughter of James VI and I, and the Privy Council levied around 50,000 Scots to take part. Most Scots fighting in the wars were under warrant or in foreign service (some as mercenaries). For quite a few Scots it was also a religious war. Many saw themselves as fighting for the Protestant cause, while others saw themselves as serving Catholicism. Scotland actually declared war on Spain (1625–1630) and France (1627–1629).

Thousands of Scottish soldiers returned and formed the muscle and leadership for both Covenanter and Royalist forces, as the chaos and bloodshed of the European war tipped over into The Wars of the Three Kingdoms in Britain and Ireland (see The Harrowing of the Campbell Lands, below). In 1644, the parliamentary 'Army of Both Kingdoms' was led by a Scots veteran of the Thirty Years War, Alexander Leslie, as was the Royalist army, by Patrick Ruthven (who, more prosaically perhaps, became 1st Earl of Brentford).

THE HARROWING OF THE CAMPBELL LANDS (1644–5)

The British and Irish Civil Wars of 1642–6 and 1648–9 are referred to as the Wars of the Three Kingdoms. The conflicts began in Scotland with the Bishops' Wars of 1639–40 and in Ireland in 1641 with the Irish Catholic rebellion in Ulster. The fighting in Scotland was especially bloody, with deep sectarian, national, and clan hatreds erupting all over. The Ulster Catholic hero Alisdair MacColla landed in Scotland in 1644, and threw his Irish troops behind the Earl of Montrose's campaign against the king's enemies in Scotland, the Protestant Covenanters and their (largely Campbell) Highland allies. MacColla's men captured Aberdeen in 1644 in a storm of rape, murder, and looting that lasted for three days. This event horrified many Scots, and did great harm to Montrose's cause. As is often noted, MacColla's agenda differed from Montrose's: Montrose was fighting a British civil war, whereas MacColla was fighting for Clan Donald against the old Campbell enemy.

In December 1644 MacColla descended upon the Campbell lands in Argyll, slaughtering hundreds of civilians and burning their homes. In February 1645, at Inverlochy, he routed a Covenanter army consisting of Lowland troops and Campbells. Throughout MacColla's campaign, his troops were given leave to plunder and kill the Campbells. The worst of his atrocities, 'the Barn of Bones', occurred in Laganmor, where the glen's defenceless women and children were imprisoned in a barn and burned alive. Atrocity followed atrocity. After the Battle of Philliphaugh in 1645, around eighty Irish women and children were murdered by their Covenanter captors at Linlithgow. The terror wrought upon the Campbells by MacColla was to be paid for later, not by MacColla himself, who was killed In Ireland in 1647, but by his MacDonald kinsmen.

GLENCOE (1692)

Glencoe is the most famous Scottish massacre and probably the most misunderstood. The massacre came at the end of centuries of relentless clan warfare, and was carried out on a cold February night by a detachment of Campbells who had been ordered 'to fall upon the rebels, MacDonalds of Glencoe, and put all to the sword under seventy'. The Campbell contingent included many men whose close family members had been butchered and raped by MacDonalds. The Campbells were billeted on the MacDonalds and rose up in the night, killing at least thirty-eight of them: another forty died of exposure after fleeing into the bleak mountains. It has long been claimed that the massacre was particularly horrible because the Campbells committed 'murder under trust' by breaching traditional rules of hospitality, but, in truth, the massacre made an immediate impact because it was part of British, not just Highland, history, with responsibility reaching to the highest in the land, King William himself. Tory propagandists in England and Scotland (quite rightly) made sure it was not forgotten.

Two young government officers approaching the carnage broke their swords and refused to be involved. The 1695 Commission of Enquiry into the massacre effectively backed the two officers, and established an important principle in British and international law, stating that 'no command against the law of nature is binding; so that a soldier, retaining his commission, ought to refuse to execute any barbarity'. This judgement remains a vital legal precedent.

8

The Scottish Enlightenment

❖

On Edinburgh's High Street, directly opposite St Giles Cathedral, stands the Mercat (Market) Cross, the old High Street centre of the city. During the extraordinary eighteenth-century efflorescence of learning, arts, and culture that we call the Scottish Enlightenment, this cross was the site for royal proclamations and also the place to stand and watch the notables of the city pass by. The High Street was home to many writers, soldiers, philosophers, and scholars.

William Smellie (1740–95), printer to the University of Edinburgh and editor of the first edition of the *Encyclopaedia Britannica* (1768–71), claimed that an English visitor to Edinburgh observed: 'Here I stand at what is called the Cross of Edinburgh, and can, in a few minutes, take fifty men of genius and learning by the hand.'

A generally accepted timescale for the Enlightenment would date from the publication of David Hume's *A Treatise of Human Nature* in 1739, to the publication of James Hutton's *Theory of the Earth* in 1795. Learning in Scotland had always been valued (by law, from 1616, every parish had to have a school), and by the early eighteenth century the nation's universities were hotbeds of enquiry. In order of founding, the four Scottish universities designated as 'ancient' that existed prior to the eighteenth century are:

University of St Andrews (founded 1413)

University of Glasgow (founded 1451)

University of Aberdeen (Aberdeen had two universities, **King's College**, founded 1495, and **Marischal College**, founded 1593; the colleges merged to form a united University of Aberdeen in 1860)

University of Edinburgh (founded 1583)

The precise reasons for the sudden historical wave of genius are still debated. Scottish nationalists have tended to play down the Act of Union in 1707 as an influence, but there can be little doubt that the added British dimension extended and enriched the Scottish cultural experience (while also diluting some aspects, such as the use of the Scots language in 'polite' society). The market for plays, novels, and histories expanded, as did the company with whom one could discuss ideas: Scottish intellectuals became a major force not just in London, but in every capital in Europe. By 1762 Voltaire could say, 'We look to Scotland for all our ideas of civilisation' and 'it is from Scotland that we get rules of taste in all the arts, from epic poetry to gardening'.

The Scottish Enlightenment was, above all, a practical, empirical approach to learning: the function of philosophy, of the human spirit of enquiry, was to make the world a better, more rational and more understandable place, in all aspects of the arts, and sciences. The guiding principle of the Scottish Enlightenment was that of the opening words of the English poet Alexander Pope's *An Essay on Man* (1733–4):

> Know then thyself, presume not God to scan;
> The proper study of Mankind is Man.

Plac'd on this isthmus of a middle state,
A being darkly wise, and rudely great...

—— Ten Enlightenment Philosophers ——

JOSEPH BLACK (1728–99)

A chemist and physician, born in Bordeaux, Black went to Glasgow University in 1744 to study arts, but he ended up studying medicine, and transferred to Edinburgh. His thesis of 1754 was a startlingly useful one, leading to new developments in the study of causticity, and the first identification of a gas. Black returned to Glasgow University in 1756, where he taught for ten years and became friends with James Watt. Black's influence on Watt is still much debated; what is certain is that Black's practical approach to the study of chemistry led to significant industrial innovation; the fact that Scotland became a hotbed of the Industrial Revolution is due in no small measure to Black.

JAMES BURNETT, LORD MONBODDO (1714–99)

Judge, philosopher and linguist, Monboddo was born in Monboddo House, Kincardineshire. He is credited by historians of science as having been a significant precursor of Darwin, and an early proponent of adaptive evolution. Boswell records an agreeable meeting between Dr Johnson and Monboddo in 1785, with the two old codgers agreeing that things were not as they had been:

> **Johnson:** 'Learning is much decreased in England, in my remembrance.'
> **Monboddo:** 'You, sir, have lived to see its decrease in England, I its extinction in Scotland.'

Monboddo was much ridiculed for his notion that chimps and other primates were pretty much the same as humans, and argued that men, like other apes, showed signs of a 'caudal appendage' (a tail). He also made significant contributions to the evolution of languages, and was the first scholar to use language as evidence for the single origin of humanity.

ADAM FERGUSON (1723–1816)

A philosopher and historian, born in Perthshire, Ferguson was educated at Perth Grammar School and studied Greek at St Andrews, then divinity at Edinburgh. Ferguson became a chaplain to the Black Watch and was possibly at the Battle of Fontenoy in 1745. He returned to Edinburgh in 1756, where David Hume described him as 'a Man of Sense, knowledge, Taste, Elegance, & Morals'. In 1764 Ferguson was appointed to the Chair of Pneumatics ['Mental' Philosophy] and Moral Philosophy at Edinburgh University (a post Hume had applied for twenty years previously). In religion, Ferguson aligned himself with the moderates and supported the theatre to the extent of appearing as Lady Randolph in a production of John Home's play *Douglas*. He also cleverly defended James Macpherson by saying that the Ossian epic 'appeared to me matter of some curiosity in the history of mankind, but very little as matter of vanity to one corner of this island, much less of jealousy to any other corner of it'. In 1767 Ferguson published what is still regarded as his most important work, *An Essay on the History of Civil Society*, in which he sought to reconcile the old standards of civic virtue with the new commercial world: the greatest danger for society, he said, lay in apathy and detachment. The citizen at all levels – the 'man of the world' – must be involved in the ordering of society.

DAVID HUME (1711–76)

The philosopher, historian, and political economist was born in Edinburgh, and was related to the aristocratic Home family (he changed his name from 'Home' to 'Hume' in his twenties). He attended Edinburgh University at the age of twelve to study classics. The 1911 *Britannica* describes him impeccably as 'a man of placid and even phlegmatic temperament, he lived moderately in all things, and sought worldly prosperity only so far as was necessary to give him leisure for his literary work' (a bit less impeccably, perhaps, it also describes him as 'English'). Plagued by ill health and exhaustion from study, Hume settled first in England in 1734, then France, where his health improved and he worked on his *Treatise of Human Nature, being an Attempt to Introduce the Experimental Method of Reasoning into Moral Subjects*, which was published in two volumes in 1739, in London. The work was received in near silence. Said Hume: 'Never literary attempt was more unfortunat… It fell dead-born from the press, without reaching such distinction as even to excite a murmur among the zealots. But,' he added, 'being naturally of a cheerful and sanguine temper, I very soon recovered the blow, and prosecuted with great ardour my studies in the country.'

In 1741–2, Hume published *Essays: Moral and Political* and in 1744 applied for the Chair of Pneumatics and Moral Philosophy at Edinburgh University. The Scottish clergymen in charge of the appointments rejected him, however, on account of his now notorious 'atheism' (Hume himself, profoundly sceptical in all things, rejected both the labels of 'atheist' and the old and increasingly unfashionable get-out term of 'deist'; most scholars now refer to him simply as 'irreligious'). Hume clearly had to be careful what he said about religion. Thomas

Aikenhead (see p. 78) had been burned alive in Edinburgh for atheism just fifteen years before Hume was born.

In 1748 he published *An Enquiry Concerning Human Understanding*, which includes the famous discussion of miracles, which set the intellectual tone for future debates on the supernatural. His silky observation that 'the Christian Religion not only was at first attended with miracles, but even at this day cannot be believed by any reasonable person without one', remains one of the great rhetorical mortar shells of all time.

Published in six volumes between 1754 and 1762, Hume's huge *The History of Great Britain* (subsequently called *The History of England*) established him as one of the great historians of the age. The million-word work was greatly admired by his peers, and popular with the public. Other works include *The Natural History of Religion* (1757) and the posthumous *Dialogues Concerning Natural Religion* (1779).

The nineteenth-century philosopher James Hutchison Stirling summed up Hume's intellectual legacy thus: 'Hume is our Politics, Hume is our Trade, Hume is our Philosophy, Hume is our Religion.'

WILLIAM HUNTER (1718–83) and JOHN HUNTER (1728–93)

The Hunter brothers were born in East Kilbride. William Hunter studied divinity at Glasgow University but (in a not unusual progression) went on to practise medicine in 1737 in London, becoming physician to Queen Charlotte. He was Professor of Anatomy at the Royal Academy of Arts, 1769–72 (and has been credited with rediscovering Leonardo da Vinci's drawings in the royal collection, which he used as aids for anatomical study). Hunter's huge collection of biological and ethnographic material was bequeathed to Glasgow University, and can be seen at the Hunterian Museum and Art Gallery.

John Hunter practised medicine in London with his brother and became an army surgeon, 1760–3. He was appointed surgeon to King George III in 1776, and Surgeon General in 1789. Though he had little formal education, Hunter made several major contributions to medical science, especially in obstetrics. He stood out from his contemporaries, a fact of which he was sadly too aware: an acquaintance noted that Hunter was 'deficient in those refined gentlemanly feelings, and those conciliatory manners… especially requisite in the medical profession. Conscious of great mental superiority, he was too apt to show this in a rude and overbearing manner.' He may have died from a heart attack brought on by an argument.

FRANCIS HUTCHESON (1694–1746)

The philosopher was born in County Down, Ulster (his family were originally from Ayrshire). Hutcheson studied classics and theology at Glasgow University from 1710, and eventually returned to Dublin, where he opened an academy and published four essays (all published anonymously, though their authorship was an open secret), including his best known work, *An Inquiry into the Original of our Ideas of Beauty and Virtue* (1725). He argued for an 'internal sense' concerned with beauty and order, and for 'moral sense' enabling one to recognize benevolence in action: 'Wisdom denotes the pursuing of the best ends by the best means'; 'That action is best, which procures the greatest happiness for the greatest numbers'.

Hutcheson became Professor of Moral Philosophy in 1729 at Glasgow University, a position he made one of great influence, and held until his death in 1746. He was involved in the

New Light religious revival movement, which promoted more liberal views on religion than those advanced by Scotland's Calvinist establishment and taught in English rather than in Latin. Hutcheson was greatly influential on his student Adam Smith and on later utilitarians such as Jeremy Bentham.

JAMES HUTTON (1726–97)

A geologist, he was born in Edinburgh. Hutton's study of Scottish geology convinced him that the earth was much older than it was thought to be: he was not the first person to think this, but he was certainly the first to demonstrate the truth of the assertion using scientific principles, and he is regarded as the founder of geology as a science. Hutton studied at Edinburgh University and in Paris, and made a fortune as a partner in a business extracting ammonium chloride (which has many industrial uses) from the soot produced by Edinburgh's many chimneys.

Hutton farmed in Norfolk and the Borders, and became a shareholder in and manager of the Forth and Clyde Canal project. An active member of the Royal Society of Edinburgh after its formation in 1783, in 1785 he read a paper to the society entitled 'Theory of the earth, or, An investigation of the laws observable in the composition, dissolution, and restoration of land upon the globe', which was the first expression of his theory.

Hutton's subsequent studies of sedimentary layers were brought together in *Theory of the Earth* (1795), in which he showed that only a huge expanse of time (what became known as 'deep time') could have produced such an outcome: 'Here are three distinct successive periods of existence, and each of these is, in our measurement of time, a thing of infinite duration ... The result, therefore, of this physical inquiry is, that we find no vestige of a beginning, no prospect of an end.' Hutton's friend John Playfair described the impact of Hutton's theory: 'the mind seemed to grow giddy looking so far into the abyss of time.'

THOMAS REID (1710–96)

Natural and moral philosopher, born in Strachan, Kincardine-shire, Reid attended Aberdeen Grammar School, and went to the city's Marischal College in 1723 to study philosophy. Reid became a professor at the city's King's College in 1752, and in 1764 published his *Inquiry into the Human Mind, on the Principles of Common Sense*, a work that is regarded as the founding text of what became known as the 'Scottish School of Common Sense'. Reid's theory was based upon 'six axioms', which began with the observation that the thoughts of which we are conscious are the thoughts of an independent mind. 'Common sense' is open to all, we are ruled by common sense, and philosophical paradoxes are just word games. The school was attacked by Kant and others, on the common-sense ground that it seemed as if common-sense philosophers were simply reactive (and uncommonly argumentative), but Reid's theories remained hugely influential in the nineteenth century.

ADAM SMITH (1723–90)

Economist and moral philosopher, born in Kirkcaldy, he was the only major future philosopher to be abducted by gypsies (at the age of three or four; he was swiftly rescued). He attended Glasgow University aged fourteen where he was taught moral philosophy by Francis Hutcheson. Smith went to Balliol, Oxford, in 1740, and his experience there is often used as an example of the differences between the Scottish and English universities of the day: as the *Dictionary of National Biography* puts it, his sympathies were 'whig, Presbyterian, and Hanoverian', and he could not possibly be sympathetic to the 'tory, high-church, and Jacobite sympathies of Balliol'.

Smith returned to Scotland where he became acquainted with fellow intellectuals, most notably David Hume, who became a firm friend.

Smith was appointed Professor of Logic (and of Moral Philosophy) at Glasgow University in 1751, and published *The Theory of Moral Sentiments* in 1759. Smith's gift for vivid imagery electrified his contemporaries: 'In ease of body, peace of mind, all the different ranks of life are nearly upon a level and the beggar who suns himself by the side of the highway possesses that security which kings are fighting for.'

Smith's major work is *An Inquiry into the Nature and Causes of the Wealth of Nations* (1776), now regarded as the founding text of political economy, covering such topics as value, the division of labour, and the operation of the free market both nationally and internationally. Again, the text is shot through with lucid, compelling illustration:

> It is not from the benevolence of the butcher, the brewer, or the baker, that we expect our dinner, but from their regard to their own interest. We address ourselves, not to their humanity but to their self-love, and never talk to them of our own necessities but of their advantages… Nothing is more useful than water: but it will purchase scarce any thing; scarce any thing can be had in exchange for it. A diamond, on the contrary, has scarce any value in use; but a very great quantity of other goods may frequently be had in exchange for it.

Smith is claimed as one of their own by socialists, liberals, and conservatives, and the Labour Prime Minister Gordon Brown asserted a special affinity with Smith as both were from Kirk-caldy. The Glasgow-born, Kirkcaldy-raised Brown has said (on several occasions): 'Coming from Kirkcaldy, I have come to understand that his *Wealth of Nations* was underpinned by his *Theory of the Moral Sentiments*...'

—— Three Enlightenment Engineers ——

ROBERT STEVENSON (1772–1850)

A civil engineer, he was born in Glasgow. Robert Stevenson's mother intended him for the ministry, but at the tender age of nineteen he was given the task (by his uncle, engineer to the Northern Lighthouse Board) of supervising the construction of a lighthouse on Little Cumbrae in the Clyde. Stevenson found his vocation, and decided to be a civil engineer and build lighthouses. He combined studies at Glasgow's Andersonian Institute with building a lighthouse in Orkney, and also attended lectures at Edinburgh University. In 1797, aged twenty-five, he was appointed engineer to the Northern Lighthouse Board, succeeding his uncle. Stevenson's aptitude for building lighthouses was recognized in his own time as being of the greatest importance: as a result of his work, many lives were saved, shipping became safer, and trade made easier. His greatest work is the Bell Rock Lighthouse, east of Arbroath, which still stands today and is the world's oldest sea-washed lighthouse.

Stevenson worked with many other engineers of the day, including Thomas Telford. Three of his sons became engineers: David, Alan, and Thomas. Robert Stevenson was the grandfather (through Thomas) of Robert Louis Stevenson. See *The Lighthouse Stevensons* (1999), by Bella Bathurst.

Thomas Telford (1757–1834)

Architect, civil engineer, and stonemason, Telford was born in Westerkirk, Eskdale. Raised in poverty but not despair (his nickname was 'Laughing Tam'), he was apprenticed at the age of fourteen to a stonemason, but his career progressed rapidly. In London, in 1782, he received the support of Robert Adam. In 1787 Telford was appointed Surveyor of Public Works in Shropshire, where he built around forty bridges. In 1804–22, he worked on the huge project of the Caledonian Canal, and worked on at least thirty-three of the canals that criss-crossed the industrial landscape. As well as canals and bridges (Dean Bridge in Edinburgh is probably the loveliest, the Menai Bridge the most impressive), he also built vitally needed roads all over the country.

James Watt (1736–1819)

Engineer and scientist, born in Greenock to a prominent local merchant family, and described as 'slow' at Greenock Grammar School, Watt spent a year in London in 1755–6 as an instrument maker. On his return to Glasgow, academic friends got him a position, with a small workshop, in 1758 as 'mathematical instrument maker to the university'. His friends there now included Joseph Black; Black explained to Watt what was happening during the 'tea kettle' experiment, and clearly there was a heady atmosphere of theory and practice at the university. Black's successor as chemistry lecturer, John Robison, described meeting Watt for the first time thus: 'I saw a workman ... but was surprised to find a philosopher as young as myself and always ready to instruct me ... everything became to him a subject of new and serious study. Everything became science in his hands.' (Robison suggested to Watt, in 1759, that steam power could be developed for mining and 'road carriage' use.)

Watt subsequently became rich, successful in industry, and his developments and innovations in steam power drove the Industrial Revolution forward.

—— A Partnership in Social Engineering ——

DAVID DALE (1739–1806) and ROBERT OWEN (1771–1858)
David Dale's Glasgow tombstone simply says 'David Dale, Merchant', but he was much more than that. Apprenticed to the weaving trade in Paisley, Dale set up on his own in 1763 as a linen dealer, and like many Nonconformists of the period combined piety with profit (in his case sincerely). In 1784 Dale founded the cotton mill village of New Lanark on the Clyde, with Richard Arkwright as his partner. New Lanark – a business run on humanitarian lines – was a tourist attraction as early as the 1790s, as the visitors' book confirms (about 750 signatures a year). Dale provided clean and healthy living conditions, education, and good food, and also took apprentices from urban poorhouses (and encouraged country dancing, but for exercise rather than flirting). He taught himself Greek and Hebrew, and gave over £50,000 to charity.

In 1799 he sold New Lanark to the Welsh philanthropist Robert Owen, who married his eldest daughter, Ann Caroline. Somewhat unfairly, Owen is the man most people associate with New Lanark, rather than Dale. Owen was mill manager, 1800–26, and continued Dale's good work. Opening the rather stern-sounding Institute for the Formation of Character in 1816, Owen stated: 'I know that society may be formed so as to exist without crime, without poverty; with health greatly improved, with little, if any misery, and with intelligence and happiness increased a hundredfold.' New Lanark is a UNESCO World Heritage Site.

9

RELIGION

❖

—— The Old Gods ——

Despite the best endeavours of legions of New Agers, we know very little of the old pre-Christian religions of Britain. The Romans were fascinated by Druidism, and it has been suggested that some Romans may have travelled into Caledonia for insights into the religion (like hippies visiting 1960s India), but, sadly, descriptions of any such trips are lacking.

The scrappy evidence the Romans have left us tends to suggest, along with the evidence of sacrificial burials found in peat bogs in Ireland and southern Britain, that it is unlikely that pre-Christian Iron Age Caledonia was a land in which the gods were kind; *The Wicker Man* may be as valid a guide to the old religion as anything we have.

ST NINIAN *(fl. fifth to sixth centuries)*
We can be fairly sure there were Christians in Roman Scotland, whether serving in the legions or trading with the forts and the tribesmen, or shivering on Hadrian's Wall with Auden's sentry in 'Roman Wall Blues': 'Piso's a Christian, he worships a fish' (the fish of course was a symbol for Christ in Roman times).

The first missionary into Scotland we have knowledge of is St Ninian. The accepted wisdom used to be that Ninian was Scotland's Apostle: a native of Cumbria who was sent by

Rome to convert the Picts. But scholars now believe that there may have been two Ninians; or indeed that a scribe of the old Church mixed him up with one of Columba's mentors, and that he is really just a spelling mistake. It has also been suggested that Ninian's life may be a fabrication designed to bolster some clerical power struggle.

Church tradition associates Ninian with the foundation at Whithorn, but the association remains a matter of legend rather than fact. No fifth-century archaeological remains have been found at Whithorn, which spoilsports say may originally have been a sixth-century Irish monastic settlement. Ninian was also known as Trinnean, and St Trinnean's School in Edinburgh is supposed to have been the inspiration for Ronald Searle's fictional St Trinian's.

PATRICK (fl. fifth century)

Christianity retained a presence among Britons after the Romans left, and Patrick's family were among those Christians; his father was a deacon called Calpornius. We include Patrick here, as one of the traditional birthplaces for him is Dumbarton, among the Strathclyde Britons, at the very western end of the Antonine Wall. Patrick was kidnapped by Irish slavers when a boy, and escaped after about six years. He became a priest – eventually a bishop – and returned to Ireland to preach the gospel. The *Dictionary of National Biography* states confidently that Patrick's mission to Ireland 'can be securely dated to the 5th century'. Patrick's *Confession* is a much studied work for clues about clerical tensions of the time; his emphasis on grace may indicate that he was a Roman loyalist at a time when many Christians were influenced by the teachings of that very British heretic and denier of original sin, Pelagius. Though Patrick was never formally canonized, he was recognized as Ireland's patron saint by at least the eighth century.

COLUMBA (c.521–97)

Whether or not Ninian existed, the Abbot Finnian of Clonard in Ireland certainly existed, as did Columba.

Columba started the first copyright war in publishing history after he illegally copied one of Finnian's prized psalters. This theft of what we now call 'intellectual property rights' led to the Battle of Cooldrevny in 561, in which 3,000 warriors may have died. Overcome with remorse, Columba left Ireland to preach the gospel to the Picts, and landed on Iona in 563. Iona was a good strategic base for these missionaries, halfway between the territory of the Scots of Dalriada and the great Pictish lands to the east.

According to his biographer, Adamnan, it was possibly while on a journey to Inverness to meet the Pictish king Bridei that Columba came across Picts burying a man by the River Ness, who had been killed by a monster in the river. Columba sent one of his own enthusiastic followers into the river as bait: the monster attacked but fled when Columba ordered it to leave his servant alone. This account is of doubtful historical merit as Nessie, who was presumably on her way into or out of Loch Ness, seems shy and peaceful, and has never attacked anyone else.

The Venerable Bede suggests, about 200 years later, that Bridei gifted Iona to Columba, who converted the king to Christianity. The gift of Iona is not mentioned by Adamnan, who suggests that Bridei was only nice to Columba after the saint performed one of his customary miracles. Neither does

Adamnan claim that Bridei was converted by Columba; Bridei may well have been a Christian already (see p. 45).

Columba died peacefully in Iona in 597. His legacy was huge. Iona became one of the most important missionary centres in Europe and is itself now a place of pilgrimage. The great illuminated manuscript, The Book of Kells, which was made around 800 and now lives in Trinity College, Dublin, was possibly created on Iona (or in England, or, indeed, Ireland).

THE 'CELTIC CHURCH'

Ulster and Scottish Presbyterians, feminists and liberation theologians have all been keen to emphasize the distinct nature of Columba's 'Celtic Church' and lament its being 'taken over' by Roman authority at the Synod of Whitby (664). Liberals imagine a lost 'Celtic Church' concerned with sexual equality, democracy, and general caring and sharing that seems difficult to reconcile with what we actually know of Columba's disputative, status-hungry monks. Ian Paisley's vision of Christians taking their guidance directly from God seems closer to the mark, but is still a case of projecting the present into the past. You picks up your hymn book, and you takes your choice.

—— The 'Dark' and Middle Ages ——

By the eleventh century, the Roman Catholic Church was apparently firmly in control, with Macbeth making at least one pilgrimage to Rome. And our Scottish bishops seem to have been no more notably corrupt or violent or pious than bishops anywhere. Scotland produced a fair number of saints, if not quite on the industrial scale of Ireland. Some notable pre-Reformation figures are listed below.

St Kessog *(died c.560)*

Kessog was a follower of Columba. One of the early martyrs in Scotland, he was Scotland's first patron saint, lived on a pretty Loch Lomond isle, and is said to have been killed by brigands.

St Donan *(died c.600)*

Donan is completely obscure, but is worthy of note as he is one of the few missionary monks of his time whose names are remembered. He may have been killed by Picts on the isle of Eigg. His name lives on in Eilean Donan.

St Kentigern *or* St Mungo *(died c.603)*

Kentigern founded the see of Glasgow, *c.*518. A Strathclyde Briton of noble descent, he is said to have been visited by Columba in the early 580s (they exchanged hugs and staffs). He is buried under Glasgow Cathedral.

St Ebba *(died c.683)*

Ebba was the daughter of an Anglo-Saxon king and queen of Northumbria, and became abbess of the 'double monastery' at Coldingham (i.e. an establishment of both monks and nuns). The monks (though not the nuns) had an unsavoury reputation for lechery and drunkenness, and Ebba brought them into line; after she died they went back to their old ways. Ebba and Cuthbert were good friends, and her bones may rest with his in Durham Cathedral.

St Cuthbert *(c.634–87)*

Like his friend Ebba, Cuthbert was English and very likely didn't care too much about race, tribe, or border (he was born in Dunbar, which is now Scottish but was then Northumbrian). In the manner of the time, he served as both a soldier and a monk, before settling into a Church career. He was Prior of

Melrose, and became Bishop of Lindisfarne. His own 'pocket gospel' – the St Cuthbert Gospel of St John – can be seen at the British Library. This beautiful work is the earliest known intact western book.

ST BLATHMAC *(died c.825)*
Blathmac was Abbot of Iona, and one of the many monks butchered there by Viking raiders. He was cut to pieces on the altar after refusing to hand over relics of Columba. His name means 'Son of Flower'.

ST MARGARET OF SCOTLAND *(c.1045–93)*
Born in Hungary, Margaret was the daughter of 'Edward the Exile', heir to the English throne usurped by William the Conqueror. Margaret became Queen Consort to Malcolm III, whom she married after being romantically shipwrecked on the coast of Scotland. They had eight children. Margaret, a woman of exemplary piety, was canonized in 1251. Her uncle was also an English royal and saint, King Edward the Confessor.

ST MAGNUS OF ORKNEY *(1075–c.1115)*
The grandson of Macbeth's ally Thorfinn, Magnus was Earl of Orkney. While serving with the Norwegian king, he refused to take part in a raid on Anglesey and stayed on board the galley singing psalms. He was murdered in 1115 on Egilsay, and Orkney's great cathedral of St Magnus was built in his honour.

DUNS SCOTUS *(c.1265–1308)*
The Irish used to claim Duns Scotus, but it is now generally accepted that the man was, as his name suggests, a Scot born in the Border town of Duns. His early life before becoming a Franciscan is shrouded in obscurity, but by the beginning of the fourteenth century he was studying theology at Oxford,

Cambridge, and Paris. Dubbed the 'subtle doctor', Duns Scotus made significant contributions to the study of natural theology, moral philosophy, and ethics.

—— The Reformation ——

JOHN KNOX (1514–72)

For generations of Scots, the Scottish Reformation conjures up images of John Knox shouting at Mary, Queen of Scots. Which is fair enough: the story of John Knox is the story of the Scottish Reformation.

Born in Haddington into a family that had a tradition of service to the Bothwells, Knox converted to Protestantism in the 1540s, going into hiding shortly afterwards as persecution of the heretics spread. The Protestants – growing in numbers and conviction – fought back; Knox himself carried a broadsword. Whereas the English Reformation was Lutheran and fairly tolerant, the Scottish Reformation was Calvinist and drew its boundaries with rings of steel. In 1546 the Archbishop of St Andrews, David Beaton, was murdered in his own castle by Reformers – he was to be the last pre-Reformation cardinal in Scotland.

The French intervened on behalf of their still ruling co-religionists, and Knox ended up as a slave in the French galleys, a brutal and generally short-lived fate. Knox said he and the other Protestants stuck to their faith and claimed that he threw a picture of the Virgin Mary over the side (checking first, he honestly admits, that he was not being watched).

Knox was released from slavery in 1549, probably thanks to English influence. In England, he was given £5 by the Privy Council and sent to Berwick to preach the gospel. Knox's influence grew to the extent that he became a royal chaplain, and attracted the attention of Archbishop Cranmer, who dismissed Knox and his brethren as 'unquiet spirits'. When Protestant Edward VI died and Catholic Mary I inherited the English throne, Knox wisely kept away from London (around this time, Knox said that England meant more to him than Scotland). He went into exile in Europe, and in 1555 returned to Scotland, where he married and composed his most famous diatribe, *The First Blast of the Trumpet Against the Monstrous Regiment of Women*, a stream of invective designed to show how the rule of women was unnatural. Mary I died in 1558, and was succeeded by a Protestant, but the Protestant was a woman, Elizabeth I, and she never forgave Knox for denying women's right to rule. Knox's tract is one of the most mistimed in history.

In 1561 Mary, Queen of Scots, landed in Scotland. She had a mass said in the royal chapel, which was attacked by angry Protestants. Said Knox: 'That one Mess… was more fearful to him then gif ten thousand armed enemyes.'

Knox had four interviews with Mary, each one loaded with drama. At one point Mary, in one of the most startling diplomatic offers ever made, suggested to Knox that he could be her personal spiritual adviser. At their last interview, Mary rebuked Knox for preaching against the possibility of a Catholic husband for her, and asked him what he thought his role was in the kingdom. Knox responded: 'A subject borne within the same… Madam. And albeit I neather be Erle, Lord, nor Barroun within it… God maid me… a profitable member within the same.'

Mary wept, but Knox was unmoved – and in 1567, before she escaped to England, approved her execution as an adulteress.

By the time Knox died in 1572, many more lives than Mary's had been lost, but Scotland was under Presbyterian rule.

—— Post-Reformation Scotland ——

The history of religion in Scotland from the early sixteenth century onwards can be told in many ways, but one of the most obvious is the waning of the ability of the religious to persecute non-believers, whether 'heretics' or 'witches' or just 'unbelievers'. The seventeenth-century Protestant Covenanters were very brave men and women, who fought well for liberty as they saw it, and not just in Scotland; Scots Covenanters made a decisive contribution to Cromwell's victory at Marston Moor in 1644. But when Cromwell invaded Scotland in 1650 and defeated the Scottish army at Dunbar, there may well have been more relief than despondency in Scotland, as the tides of godly purge and counter-purge came at last to an end (see also p.79).

Disruption fractured the Protestant Churches in the nineteenth century; many of these ruptures and debates seemed of great import at the time, but few modern Scots have any interest in these lost arguments. When the Free Church in the Western Isles split apart in the 1990s, the dominant feeling was that though it was a sad affair for the communities involved, it was a matter of no great relevance for the nation.

—— Religion in Modern Scotland ——

The 2001 Government Census asked Scots what their religion was: 67 per cent said they had a religion; 65 per cent said they were Christian; of these, 42 per cent said they were Church of Scotland, 16 per Roman Catholic and 7 per cent 'other' Christian.

Those who 'wrote in' their religion as 'other' Christian included Methodist, Church of England, Orthodox, Jehovah's Witness and so on.

For other religions, 42,000 people identified themselves as Muslim; Buddhists, Sikhs, and Jews were over 6,000 each, and Hindus over 5,000. There were also 27,000 who simply registered as 'other'.

As with the rest of the UK, there was an Internet campaign encouraging people to identify themselves as 'Jedi'. Over 14,000 Scots did so.

(Information taken from Scotland's Census 2001, General Register Office for Scotland, Edinburgh, 25 March 2003.)

10

Sports and Pastimes

❖

Scotland is the home of three great sports: shinty, curling, and golf. Scots also developed the modern game of football (not 'soccer'; Scots, like others on these islands, don't use this word much). Other popular sports include rugby, cricket (yes, cricket) and various small-town rituals that involve moving a ball from one end of a town to another.

—— Shinty ——

Shinty is said to have evolved from the old Irish sport of hurling. The Highlands and Western Isles make up the shinty heartland. The game is played between two teams of players: each of the players is armed with a curved stick (a 'caman') and the objective is to hit a leather ball into the opposing team's net. The ball can travel at a speed of over 100 mph.

The world governing body is the Camanachd Association, founded in Kingussie in 1893 and based in Inverness. The association divides Scotland into two regions: north of Ballachulish and south of Ballachulish. Kingussie is far and away the most successful club in shinty history, having won the league for twenty years running. The 2005 edition of the *Guinness Book of Records* lists Kingussie as world sport's most successful club side.

Ice hockey is believed to derive from shinty, and this seems plausible; informal games of ice hockey in Canada have long been called 'shinny' which almost certainly originates from 'shinty'.

—— Curling ——

Curling is a game played on ice. Two teams of four players each compete to slide polished granite stones towards a target (called the 'house'). Each stone is preceded by two 'sweepers' with brooms who smooth the stone's voyage. It has been asserted that curling is like 'chess on ice' but this claim has only ever been made by curlers; it's more like lawn bowls on ice.

Curling goes back at the very least to 1511, which is the date carved on a stone found in a pond at Dunblane. Something very similar to curling is shown taking place in a painting by Breughel the Elder, *Winter Landscape with a Bird Trap* (1565), but Scotland's claim to be the home of curling has always been widely accepted. Kilsyth Curling Club (founded 1716) is the oldest in the world.

Curling is hardly a mass sport in Scotland, and the only country in which it has a following of any real significance is Canada. At the 2002 Olympic Winter Games, the British team won gold, to everyone's surprise. The team was composed entirely of Scots, and was Britain's first gold medal at the Winter Olympics since Torvill and Dean's 'Bolero' in 1984.

—— Golf ——

Golf is a game in which a player armed with different varieties of clubs, called 'irons' and 'woods', attempts to hit a ball into a number of holes, usually 18. If two or more golfers are playing against each other, the player who goes round the course using the least number of strokes is the winner.

Men have hit balls with sticks since the Stone Age, and there have been various attempts to identify an origin for golf from all around the world, from the Netherlands to China. However, it seems mean to deny Scotland's claim to be the game's home, as:

- the word 'golf' seems to be first recorded in a Scottish statute of 1457 among a list of games banned by King James II, in order to encourage archery practice (the word is claimed to derive from the old Scots 'golf': 'to strike out').

- the first recorded game of golf was played at Bruntsfield Links in 1456.

- the world's oldest golf course is the Musselburgh Old Links; its earliest recorded match was in 1672. Mary, Queen of Scots, is also supposed to have played golf here in 1567 (a claim as convincing as any other modern advertising claims about her pastimes).

- the first golfing international was played on Edinburgh's Leith Links in 1681 between Scotland and England. Scotland was represented by the Duke of York and a cobbler called John Paterson. The England team consisted of two nobles who claimed that golf was English in origin. Scotland won, and John Paterson bought a house at 77 Canongate with his share of the winnings.

- the thirteen rules that form the basis of the modern game were formulated by the Honourable Company of Edinburgh Golfers and first applied on Leith Links in 1774.

The real Scottish sport, football, is loved and played all over the land. The basic rules of the modern game were codified by England's Football Association in 1863, but the modern fluid passing game is the creation of Scots. A book called *Vocabula* written in Latin by David Wedderburn in 1633 describes a game between two teams in which players pass the ball to teammates. And in the late nineteenth century, Scots players showed the English how to play the 'beautiful game'. Here are eleven more or less 'beautiful' games of football.

1885: ARBROATH 36 BON ACCORD 0
The result of this Scottish Cup tie, between an experienced Arbroath and an amateur team from Aberdeen, is still a world-record victory in a senior game of football. On the same day, Dundee Harp beat Aberdeen Rovers 35–0.

1961: ENGLAND 9 SCOTLAND 3
The great Scottish sports commentator Arthur Montford often had reason to utter his famous words 'Disaster for Scotland!', and one of the worst disasters for Scotland was this 9–3 defeat at Wembley. The goalkeeper was called Frank Haffey and the joke went: 'What's the time?' – 'Nearly ten past Haffey'.

1963: ENGLAND 1 SCOTLAND 2
One of Scotland's greatest victories against England. Scotland played most of the match with just ten men, after the captain Eric Caldow was taken off with a broken leg (no substitutes were allowed in those days). Jim Baxter scored both goals, the second from the first penalty he ever took.

(April) 1967: England 2 Scotland 3

In April 1967 England were world champions with an unbeaten run of nineteen wins prior to the match, and Scotland were most definitely underdogs; England had very fine players but so did Scotland: four of the Celtic team who would in the following month lift the European Cup; two of the Rangers players who would lose the Cup-Winners Cup in the same month to Bayern Munich; and three of Scotland's greatest ever players: Jim Baxter, Billy Bremner, and Denis Law. Scotland were worthy winners.

(May) 1967: Celtic 2 Inter Milan 1

As all but the most die-hard of Rangers fans will agree, this is the most beautiful game of them all, the European Cup final of 1967. The Italians played an ugly form of defensive football, the dreaded *'catenaccio'* ('door bolt') defensive system. The Scots attacked in force and came from behind to win the match 2–1 and become the first British club to win the European Cup. The Inter manager said, 'Celtic deserved to win and their win was a victory for the sport.' The Celtic players were Ronnie Simpson in goal, Jim Craig, Tommy Gemmell, Bobby Murdoch, Billy McNeill (captain), John Clark, Jimmy Johnstone, William Wallace, Stevie Chalmers, Bertie Auld, and Bobby Lennox. The 'Lisbon Lions' were all born within a thirty-mile radius of Glasgow, and we shall never see their like again.

1971: Partick Thistle 4 Celtic 1

The reports of a convincing Celtic victory were apparently being written before the game, the final of the Scottish League Cup, took place. Celtic were strong favourites, but the famously unpredictable Jags didn't just win, they won well. The victory is still one of the major upsets in Scottish football.

1972: RANGERS 3 DYNAMO MOSCOW 2

Rangers defeated Dynamo Moscow in the Cup-Winners Cup final in Barcelona and thus won their only European trophy. It is perhaps an exaggeration to call this match a beautiful game as the Rangers fans invaded the pitch and the Spanish police waded into them with batons. Bottles were thrown by some Rangers fans, and the club was banned from Europe for two years. One of the Rangers team was Alfie Conn, who is still one of the very few men to have played for both Celtic and Rangers.

1978: SCOTLAND 3 HOLLAND 2

After a terrible draw with Iran, Scotland needed to beat Holland by three goals to progress in this World Cup tournament in Argentina. The Scots were leading 2–1 when midfielder Archie Gemmill (one of the smallest players on the pitch) pounced on the ball, did a one-two with Dalglish then swanned gracefully into the box and hit the ball past the goalkeeper. For many Scots, it is still the best goal they ever saw, but alas, a goal of no significance as a few minutes later Johnny Rep scored for Holland. The team was managed by Ally MacLeod, who was reviled as extravagantly by the Scots after the tournament as he was praised before it.

1983: ABERDEEN 2 REAL MADRID 1

Aberdeen rose from obscurity in the early 1980s to become one of the major teams in Europe. Managed by Alex Ferguson and captained by Willie Miller, this was the team's finest moment – defeating the great Real Madrid in the final of the Cup-Winners Cup.

1984: DUNDEE UNITED 2 ROMA 0

In the early 1980s the increasingly successful Dundee United (managed by Jim McLean) and Aberdeen were dubbed the

'New Firm' – the north-east of Scotland's answer to the Old Firm. It didn't last long, sadly, but there were some great games along the way, including this one, United's victory over Roma in the semi-final of the European Cup. United lost the return match 3–0. United have been drawn twice against Barcelona in European competitions; they won all four games.

2000: CELTIC 1 INVERNESS CALEDONIAN THISTLE 3

Although Caledonian Thistle – a club formed in 1994 after the merger of two Inverness clubs – had rapidly acquired a reputation as giant killers, Celtic were usually unbeatable at home, and had a great record in the Scottish Cup. However, it was the Inverness team that won the day in this cup tie, and inspired one of the greatest sporting headlines ever, created by a genius of a sub working for the Scottish edition of the *Sun*: 'Super Caley Go Ballistic, Celtic Are Atrocious'.

There was also another remarkable match – between Celtic and Dumbarton – which occurred in the context of Buffalo Bill's trip to Glasgow in 1891.

BUFFALO BILL IN GLASGOW

When Buffalo Bill took his Wild West show to Glasgow in 1891, Celtic and Rangers were already the two big draws in the city. Despite the show being based near the Celtic ground in Parkhead, Bill chose to go to Ibrox and watch Rangers play Queens Park in the Glasgow Cup. Bill wore a white sombrero which he waved at the crowd, who cheered back. Rangers were beaten 3–0 before a capacity crowd of 12,000 (sixpence to get in, and ladies got in free).

Bill never did go to see Celtic, though he did send a team of cowboys to play Celtic in a friendly – they were soundly beaten. And on New Year's Day 1892 he sent his press agent, Major

John M. Burke, to kick off the Celtic–Dumbarton game being held that day at Parkhead. The flamboyant Major Burke was cheered wildly, but there were no more loud cheers that day – Celtic were beaten 8–0, which is likely to remain the club's record home defeat. The press reports of the match gracefully tiptoe around allegations that several of the Celtic players were suffering the after-effects of a late night; and it is said that Celtic's goalkeeper may have been an Orangeman.

The drink got to Bill's Indians too. A Lakota called Charging Thunder got fighting drunk (he claimed his lemonade had been spiked), clobbered a colleague and ended up in Glasgow's Barlinnie Jail. (Charging Thunder later changed his name to George Williams and settled in Manchester, where he became a cinema usher and raised a family.)

—— Rugby ——

As is the case elsewhere, there are two forms of rugby: rugby union and rugby league, with rugby union by far the most popular in Scotland. The world's oldest continuing rugby fixture (first played in 1858) is that between pupils of Merchiston Castle School and Edinburgh Academy. Members of Edinburgh Academy made up the Scotland side in the world's first rugby international, England v. Scotland in 1871.

Rugby is an oddly distributed game in Scotland. It is a favourite game of the middle classes and their nice schools throughout the nation, but only has a broad class base in the Borders, where a brawny farm hand may lock shoulders in the scrum with the lawyer who got him off for assault in Hawick; elsewhere, it is generally only members of the professions who get to wrap their arms around each other publicly.

The stadium of the national rugby team is at Murrayfield, and national games attract much larger crowds than club games.

—— Cricket ——

The first Scottish football international was played in 1872 at the West of Scotland Cricket Ground. Oddly, in America baseball was also nurtured at cricket grounds, and the two great cuckoos of football and baseball have long since turned their backs on the foster parent. Cricket is not a sport associated with Scots, yet Scotland's favourite cartoon character – Oor Wullie in the *Sunday Post* – regularly played cricket (one of several baffling things about Wullie for Glaswegian kids).

The first recorded Scottish cricket match was in Alloa in 1785, and the first recorded contest between Scots and English was in 1865, when a Scotland team beat Surrey by 172 runs. It is a little-known fact that several Scottish sports commentators are closet cricket fans, and the renowned Bob Crampsey is openly a cricket enthusiast; indeed he wrote a fine cricket novel (albeit with an embarrasing sex scene), *The Run-Out* (1985), and quiz books about Somerset and Surrey cricket.

The wee Fife village of Freuchie earned a place in cricketing history in 1985, when its cricket team won the village cricket championship at Lord's.

—— Other Rowdy Pastimes ——

Until well into the nineteenth century, many old Scottish festivals were associated with eye-poppingly violent activities. On Whitsun Monday, for instance, the Glasgow mob took over the central riverside part of the city, driving the forces of the law away. Another popular Glasgow pastime was 'stonebricking' in which gangs from north and south of the Clyde would gather at the bridge in Stockwell Street to hurl rocks at each other. Over time, such activities became moderated into more stylized contests, with balls being used instead of bricks.

KIRKWALL BA' GAME

The Kirkwall Ba' game in Orkney is played out every Christmas Day and New Year's Day between two teams made up of those born north of the cathedral (Doonies) and those born south of the cathedral (Uppies). The object of the game is to get a leather ball from one side of Kirkwall to the other. Surprisingly, serious injuries are rare and unsporting behaviour is frowned upon. Injuries to spectators have been known to happen.

JEDBURGH BA' GAME

The object of the Jedburgh (or Jethart) Ba' Game is the same as the Kirkwall one, to get the ball from one end of the town to the other: the two teams are also called Uppies and Doonies. The Jedburgh version of this ancient pastime possibly had a macabre origin: it could be that the game was originally played with the severed heads of Border reivers.

11

Food and Drink

❖

FOOD

Scottish cuisine never used to be highly rated, not even in Scotland, which is odd, as Scotland is regarded by chefs everywhere as the source of some of the world's finest food. (NB: the use of the old term for the Scottish people, 'Scotch', is now generally reserved for Scotch food and drink, as this is what the Scots themselves prefer.) Scotland is also widely known for one world-famous offal food, haggis, and we might as well get the haggis over with at the beginning of this section.

—— Haggis ——

'Chopped heart and lungs. Boiled in a wee sheep's stomach. Tastes as good as it sounds'
GROUNDSKEEPER WILLIE, *The Simpsons*

'My mother used to say, "What do you want to eat?" and I don't ever remember saying, "Haggis, Mom"'
GEORGE BUSH, GLENEAGLES, 2005

Haggis has had a bad press. But if you're not a veggie, what's wrong with haggis? Lots of national cuisines use offal to create great dishes. There is, perhaps, just something about haggis. Haggis is not, in fact, unique to Scotland. In fact, the earliest printed references to haggis are in fifteenth-century English recipe books – 'Hacke alle togeder with gode persole [parsley]'. Controversy rages about its origins. Some say it was brought by the Romans, others by the Vikings. The truth is that there are very similar 'haggis' recipes throughout the world: only the Scottish version is regarded as both comic and disgusting, for some reason. There are of course several good brands of ready-made haggis, but if you are American you will only get American-made haggis, as most haggis is not allowed to be imported into the US (the lungs are the issue). But you can get excellent Scotch vegetarian haggis, which quite a few carnivores prefer to the offal version.

How to Make Haggis

This is an old recipe and should be followed in the imagination only.

Ask an old Scottish butcher for a Scottish sheep's stomach lining, heart, lungs, and liver. Wash them and leave overnight. Next morning, wash the stuff again (if you find a windpipe, dump it). Meanwhile, chop up two large onions, and mix with some suet, Scotch oatmeal, salt, and pepper. Boil the lining for several hours. Chop the meat, add to the suet mixture, and boil for half an hour, and (when cooled) stuff the lining with the meat. Be glad this is all a fantasy.

—— Other Scotch Delights ——

If you attend a football match in Scotland, you will find that the most popular snack at half time is a **Scotch pie**, a greasy pie filled with minced mutton. The best Scotch pies may be beef-filled and bear no culinary relation to the football pies. Another popular snack is a **bridie**, a flaky pastry filled with steak (or at the cheap end, 'steak') and optional onions. The best bridies are made in Forfar. In 2008 Scotland's master bakers complained that a lack of apprentices meant that the old mysteries associated with the production of Scotch pies and bridies may become extinct. Pies have been in trouble before: they were actually condemned by the Bishop of St Andrews in 1430 as a 'wicked' English indulgence and only the gentry were allowed them, and then only on feast days.

Probably the most popular form of sausage in Scotland is the **square (or Lorne) sausage**. All butchers have their own secret recipe (they don't want you to know, and you don't want to know), but it is always square except when it is round. The square form is designed to fit square Scotch white bread slices; the round form is for Scotch morning rolls. **Fried bread** exists in most cultures, but the Scotch (and related Ulster) version needs to be white bread and needs to be fried in lard. **Deep-fried Mars bars** are often held to be mythical, but do in fact exist in Scottish chip shops, dipped in batter and fried in the deep fryer. **Deep-fried pizza** is another Scottish chip-shop favourite. The pizzas have to be fairly small and doughy, so the frier has something to grab with the tongs that won't fall back into the fat. **Mince and tatties** remains a standard working-class dinner. The Aberdeen **buttery** is a roll which should really be called a 'lardy' as the authentic version has a high lard content.

A Scotch egg, a hard-boiled egg surrounded by sausage meat and breadcrumbs and then deep-fried, sounds and tastes Scottish, but is actually a London savoury.

—— Scotland as Food Source ——

Scotland has been a prime sourcing ground for top restaurants for many years. Lobsters and other crustaceans are harvested off the Scottish coast and exported all over the world. Scottish wild salmon is highly regarded, as are our venison and game birds. Aberdeen-Angus beef, reared where the breed was developed in the north-east, fetches a high premium. Until recently, you could only really get access to the best Scottish food by eating out in London or Barcelona or Milan: now you can even eat Scottish west coast lobster in Scottish west coast restaurants.

Fish have long been smoked in Scotland as an anti-famine measure for the cruel winter months (Boswell found smoked Scottish fish for sale in eighteenth-century London). The virtues of smoked salmon are obvious, but the humble and hugely nutritious haddock has also been fairly dealt with in Scotland. The **Finnan haddie**, named after the fishing village of Finnan, is cold-smoked over peat and a favoured method of cooking is poaching in milk (you can find a vegan tofu version of Finnan haddie lurking on the web); the **Arbroath smokie** is hot-smoked and requires no further cooking.

How to Make Porridge
Try this vegan version for one:

½ pint of water
pinch of salt
2oz medium or rough organic Scotch oatmeal
1 tablespoon soya cream
1 tablespoon Scotch heather honey

Bring the water and salt to the boil, then sprinkle in the oatmeal, stirring all the time – don't let lumps form. Simmer for about 5 minutes until the oatmeal is swollen. Pour into a white china bowl and finish with soya cream and honey. Add a sliced banana for the best slow-energy-release breakfast in the world.

DRINK

Scotland has two widely recognized national drinks: whisky and Irn-Bru (actually, tea is much more popular than either but that's not as much fun to talk about). The national alcoholic drinks used to be brandy and claret, and ales of various kinds and strengths were also drunk, as were fearsome varieties of distilled spirit. In modern Scotland's Central Belt **Buckfast Tonic Wine**, a drink produced by Benedictine monks at England's Buckfast Abbey, is the reality-drowning opiate of choice for many young working-class people. No one knows why this concoction – which is a socially respectable comforter for old biddies everywhere else in the world – has taken such a hold in this part of Scotland.

—— Irn-Bru ——

Irn-Bru is a carbonated soft drink 'Made in Scotland from Girders' as their advertising used to say; a large part of Irn-Bru's success in Scotland is undoubtedly down to a tradition of clever marketing, and there is no question of the drink's appeal to Scots. The other classic slogan associated with Irn-Bru is 'Scotland's Other National Drink'.

Manufactured by Barr's, it was originally called 'Iron Brew' when it was first produced in 1901. The iron content is pretty minimal: 0.002 per cent ammonium ferric citrate.

Even Scots who never drink the stuff may have a sneaking regard for Irn-Bru, as it is one of the few 'native' drinks anywhere to have kept (for a while) market dominance over Coca-Cola.

As is the case with haggis, not all versions of Irn-Bru are allowed into the US market (the curious should search 'Irn-Bru' at the US Food and Drug Administration website). A popular myth in Scotland has it that Russians also love Irn-Bru. This is news to most Russians.

—— Ales and Beers ——

Scotland is home to a wide variety of fine 'real' and organic beers. The tale of how the Pictish recipe for heather ale was lost is told in Robert Louis Stevenson's poem 'Heather Ale: A Galloway Legend', but there is at least one good modern substitute, and several small breweries are now producing excellent new versions of ancient Scottish ales.

—— Whisky ——

'Whisky' is the correct spelling for Scotch whisky. 'Whiskey' with an 'e' is for the Irish and American varieties. Scotch whisky is distilled from malted barley grain and must be aged in wooden barrels for a minimum of three years. Caramel is the only colouring allowed. The word derives from the Gaelic '*uisge-beatha*', 'water of life'; if you say *ooshka-beh'a*, Gaelic speakers will know what you mean.

The key distinctions in Scotch are:

- **malt whisky** is whisky that is produced by distillation in a traditional pot still, and aged for years in a cask before bottling

- **single malt whisky** is malt whisky that is produced by a single distillery and is unblended with any other whisky

- **grain whisky** is the workhorse of the industry to which may be added whole grains of other cereals

- *blended whisky* combines grain and malt and is blended for a consistency desired by supermarkets and brand names

The whisky-producing regions are grouped in several ways. The groupings that (arguably) make most sense to drinkers as opposed to classifiers are:

Lowlands – the region lying south of an imaginary line running from the Clyde to the Tay

Speyside – the classic malt-producing region: takes in the Spey watershed, extends from Inverness and Aberdeen

Islands – most notably Islay, Jura and Skye

Campbeltown – the Mull of Kintyre, where once the McCartneys lived; there used to be thirty distilleries here, now there are just two

Highlands – everything north of Lowlands except Speyside, Islands and Campbeltown

—— Ten Great Distilleries and —— Their Single Malts

Descriptions of the taste of single malts abound and may be contradictory, perhaps, indeed, divorced from reality, as a whisky stored in barrels on an inland industrial site may end up being described in rhapsodic terms of Atlantic swells lashing against the cask. Malts are generally described as 'smooth', or as 'peaty', or if the distillery is on an island, having something of the sea about them. Opinion has varied down the years about adding water; it does seem to be the case that adding a small amount of water releases more flavour (and stretches out your bottle). Most Scottish distilleries welcome visitors.

AUCHENTOSHAN *(Lowland)*
Established in 1823, since when it has had six owners, the distillery employs an unusual triple distillation process and is home to one of the few remaining great Lowland malts. Describes itself as 'Glasgow's Greatest Gem'.

GLENFIDDICH *(Speyside)*
Still (2008) under family ownership, the Glenfiddich malt dates from 1887. Like the Lowland Springbank, Glenfiddich is distilled, matured and bottled on site.

GLENLIVET *(Speyside)*
The distillery was founded in 1824, and Glenlivet is one of the most popular of all brands. Owned since 2001 by the French company Pernod Ricard, which uses Glenlivet whisky in its Chivas Regal blend.

GLENMORANGIE *(Highland)*
The distillery was founded in 1843, and, as with many distilleries, illegal manufacture on site goes back a long way, in this case possibly to the Middle Ages. Glenmorangie means 'Glen of Big Meadows', but a brilliant marketing campaign for the drink described it as 'Glen of Tranquillity'.

HIGHLAND PARK *(Islands)*
Reputedly established in the 1790s, this Orkney distillery is the most northerly (by half a mile) of all Scottish distilleries. A highly rated malt.

Isle of Jura *(Islands)*

You can't miss the place where the whisky is made: the island of Jura has 160 people, 5,000 deer, and one distillery. The Jura malt comes in several varieties, and there are no bad ones. George Orwell lived here in 1946 to begin writing *1984*, and the distillery issued a twenty-one-year-old bottling in 2005 in commemoration of the novel. The Scottish Book Trust and the distillery sponsor a writer retreat programme on the island.

Laphroaig *(Islands)*

The best known of the great Islay malts, Laphroaig is often described as an 'acquired' taste as it has a definite smoky, seaweedy flavour.

Macallan *(Speyside)*

Another of the classic Speyside malts, the Macallan (aficionados like the definite article) distillery was legally recognized in 1824. A former chairman of the company, Allan Shiach, became a Hollywood screenwriter and producer under the name of Allan Scott. Shiach wrote about twenty-five screenplays, many of which seem to feature the Macallan; there is a bottle by Sutherland and Christie's bed in *Don't Look Now*.

Springbank *(Campbeltown)*

One of the few remaining distilleries that makes, matures, and bottles its own product on site – and malts its own barley. Owned by the same family since 1837.

Talisker *(Islands)*

The only distillery on Skye (first built in 1830), Talisker is heir to a long Skye tradition of legal and illegal distilling. The ideal present to take away from Skye.

Here is a little-known fact – over 70 per cent of the UK's gins are made in Scotland, including such well-kent names as Hendrick's, Gordon's and Tanqueray.

Also on the rise are a host of craft/artisanal gins such as Blackwood's Shetland Gin, Caorunn, The Botanist, Edinburgh Gin, Heather Rose, Crossbill, and Rock Rose. These gins – flavoured with local botanicals – are world class.

12

SCOTLAND IN THE MOVIES
AND ON TV

❖

—— Twenty-seven Great Films ——

1915: BIRTH OF A NATION *directed by D.W. Griffith*
A magnificent movie about the Confederate states after the
Civil War that still manages to shock with its naked racism.
There is a scene in the film in which the hero – from a good
Scots family of Camerons – launches the Ku Klux Klan with
the words: 'Here I raise the ancient symbol of an unconquered
race of men, the fiery cross of Old Scotland's hills… I quench
its flame in the sweetest blood that ever stained the sands of
Time!' Addressed to the new mass cinematic audience, this
is how the Scots were and are presented in America: proud,
king-free, priest-free, independent, brave, non-English – and
white. The movie was used by the KKK as a recruiting tool
which resulted in the rebirth of that moribund organization.
The poisonous and historically absurd linking of Scottish history with the far right in the US continues (see Appendix A,
The Declaration of Arbroath).

1935: THE THIRTY-NINE STEPS *directed by*
Alfred Hitchcock
From the novel by John Buchan. An all-time classic and one of
the great cinema pairings: Madeleine Carroll and the Prince
of Suave, Robert Donat. It also has a top tagline: 'Handcuffed

to the Girl Who Double-crossed Him'. Rannoch Moor and the Forth Rail Bridge make stand-out appearances. The 1959 version, directed by Ralph Thomas, is seen (perhaps unfairly) as a much lesser work, but has lots more Scottish scenes.

1936: MARY OF SCOTLAND directed by John Ford
The most awful tosh, this, considering the great talent involved – Katharine Hepburn as Mary, directed by Ford, and a screenplay by Dudley Nichols. The many bonkers highlights include a demented (and invented) meeting between Mary and Elizabeth I: 'I have loved as a woman loves, lost as a woman loses… My son shall sit on the throne! My son shall rule England! Still, still, I win!'

1945: I KNOW WHERE I'M GOING directed by Michael Powell and Emeric Pressburger
A great romantic story, with the two leads Wendy Hillier and Roger Livesey giving glowing performances; Mull looks wet and windy but lovely.

1948: BONNIE PRINCE CHARLIE directed by Anthony Kimmins
As with *Mary of Scotland*, this is Hollywood Scotland, and hence beyond rational discussion. David Niven's Bonnie PC accent is truly odd.

1949: WHISKY GALORE directed by Alexander Mackendrick
Based on a Compton Mackenzie novel, which in turn was based on a real incident, the 1941 shipwreck of the SS *Politician* off Eriskay, this glorious Ealing film has long been regarded as one of the best British comedies ever made. When a ship carrying Scotch whisky founders off the (fictional) island of Todday, the

islanders conspire to carry the bottles ashore under the nose of the Home Guard. It has a marvellous ending. Filmed on beautiful Barra in an incredible three months (with studio-built sets) despite appalling weather, it went £20,000 over budget, but the boss of Ealing Studios didn't complain when he saw the rushes.

1954: BRIGADOON *directed by Vincente Minnelli*
The name 'Brigadoon' likely derives from the Brig o' Doon in Ayrshire; a great musical but nothing much to do with Scotland.

1960: KIDNAPPED *directed by Robert Stevenson*
The Disney version of the Robert Louis Stevenson novel with great scenery and great cameos of lots of Scottish talent, including Finlay Currie. There is also a 1971 version of the book with Michael Caine as a fine-looking Alan Breck.

1961: GREYFRIARS BOBBY: THE TRUE STORY OF A DOG *directed by Don Chaffey*
A Disney weepie about a Skye terrier who guards his master's Edinburgh grave. Bobby's owner was a nightwatchman rather than a farm hand, but otherwise the story is largely true.

1969: RING OF BRIGHT WATER *directed by Jack Couffer*
Based on the Gavin Maxwell book about a man and his otter relocating to the West Highlands. Beautiful location shooting, especially around Seil Island.

1969: THE PRIME OF MISS JEAN BRODIE *directed by Ronald Neame*
From the Muriel Spark novel. Late 1960s Edinburgh looks

amazing. Maggie Smith (who also looks amazing) won an Oscar for her performance as MJB.

1972: MY CHILDHOOD *directed by Bill Douglas*
This is the first film in Bill Douglas's great trilogy about growing up in poverty in the Scottish mining village of Newcraighall (the other two films are *My Ain Folk*, 1973, and *My Way Home*, 1978), known collectively as the 'Bill Douglas Trilogy'. My Childhood was filmed in Newcraighall, which is a suburb of Edinburgh – a very different Edinburgh from Miss Jean Brodie's.

1973: THE WICKER MAN *directed by Robin Hardy*
A film of many delights, a truly suspenseful script, mysterious claims about dubbing – does Annie Ross really sing in the movie? – and left-field casting (Ingrid Pitt as a postmistress). The essential guide to the film is *The Wicker Man* by Allan Brown. The final sacrificial scene on Burrow Head is magnificently filmed.

1975: MONTY PYTHON AND THE HOLY GRAIL
directed by Terry Gilliam and Terry Jones
Has many scenes filmed in Scotland: Castle Stalker makes a splendid Castle Aargh.

1979: THAT SINKING FEELING *directed by*
Bill Forsyth
Also written by Bill Forsyth, whose first film this is. A charming study of teenage life in Glasgow, with fine young actors from the Glasgow Youth Theatre.

1981: CHARIOTS OF FIRE *directed by Hugh Hudson*
The true story of Scots athlete Eric Liddell and English athlete

Harold Abrahams, and their success at the 1924 Olympic Games, at which both won gold medals. Several parts of Scotland feature in the film: St Andrews beach at the beginning and end, the Sma' Glen at Crieff, and Edinburgh in between. But it is Ian Charleson's performance as the deeply religious 'Flying Scotsman' Liddell – who refuses to run on a Sunday – that catches the heart. (The title *Chariots of Fire* is taken from Parry's hymn 'Jerusalem', adapted from a beautiful William Blake lyric, which is movingly sung at the end of the film. The hymn was dropped from the Church of Scotland hymn book in 2000, because it was felt to be no longer relevant to Scotland…)

1981: GREGORY'S GIRL *directed by Bill Forsyth*
Forsyth's fine second film, this time about a young boy falling for a female footballer. Many critics have never forgiven Forsyth for not making gloomy films about working-class failure, but that's their loss. It was filmed in Cumbernauld, which was a 'New Town' built in the mid-1950s, and has been voted one of the worst places to live in Britain.

1983: LOCAL HERO *directed by Bill Forsyth*
Regarded as Forsyth's best film; this one stars Burt Lancaster as an American tycoon whose commercial plans in Scotland are stymied by a local character, whom the tycoon comes to admire. The movie was filmed on opposite sides of Scotland: Pennan in the east for the village, Morar on the west for the beach. Eerily, the film's plot began to be played out in real life in Aberdeenshire in 2006, when the American tycoon Donald Trump's plan to build a golf course was temporarily halted (see p. 71).

1986: HIGHLANDER *directed by Russell Mulcahy*

A bizarre fantasy about sword-wielding immortals which spawned three sequels and a TV series. A film of debatable merit, but it uses Scottish scenery to great effect. Glencoe (as always) looks magnificent. The Scots accent of the lead actor, Christopher Lambert, is a regular runaway winner in polls to find the worst Scottish accent in the movies.

1993: AS AN EILEAN *('FROM THE ISLAND') directed by Mike Alexander*

A young man prepares to leave his Hebridean island to go to university. Not quite up there with *The Thirty-Nine Steps*, but the film is apparently the first feature film to be made in Scots Gaelic. It was shot around Aultbea.

1995: BRAVEHEART *directed by Mel Gibson*

And produced by and starring Mel Gibson as William Wallace. Alex Salmond said the film gave the Scots their history back, but the film is a swamp of tedious error. At one point, Gibson makes a speech telling the English to march back 'stopping at every home you pass by to beg forgiveness for a hundred years of theft, rape and murder'. In fact, by 1296, when Edward I launched his campaign against the Scots, England and Scotland had been at peace (largely) for eighty years.

The film is actually both a psychodrama prowling around the depths of Gibson's psyche – see the scene where his Wallace spits out an opiate before torture – and a very traditional sort of 'Free Scot' fantasy aimed at the American market. It was filmed in Ireland (it's cheaper) as well as Scotland.

1995: LOCH NESS *directed by John Henderson*

A really rubbish Nessie, but the Scottish scenery looks good, if a bit mixed up (in one scene Nessie swims under Eilean Donan Castle on Loch Duich).

1995: ROB ROY *directed by Michael Caton-Jones*

Basically a fine Western shot in Glencoe. Liam Neeson is quite convincing as Rob Roy the clan leader and warrior, and also conveys something of the awful old fox's deep cunning.

1996: TRAINSPOTTING *directed by Danny Boyle*

Based on the Irvine Welsh novel, this is the film that launched the big-time movie careers of, among others, Robert Carlyle, Kelly Macdonald, and Ewan McGregor. Full of energy, wit, and drugs, it was filmed in Edinburgh and Glasgow with a good segment on Rannoch Moor (*The Fast Show* once did a sketch – 'Heroin Galore' – which was a rather good blend of *Trainspotting* and *Whisky Galore*).

2002: MORVERN CALLAR *directed by Lynne Ramsay*

Based on the novel by Alan Warner. Scottish cinema has always been male-dominated, and this movie (like *Red Road*) belongs to a very select club indeed, that of Scottish movies directed by and starring women – in this case the marvellous Samantha Morton, who sets out on a strange odyssey after her boyfriend kills himself. Filmed in and around Oban.

2002: SWEET SIXTEEN *directed by Ken Loach*

Filmed in Greenock with a typical Loach cast of mostly gifted amateurs. It has English subtitles in the US.

2006: RED ROAD *directed by Andrea Arnold*

A young CCTV operator spots a man she used to know through her monitor and makes contact with him. Trouble ensues. Filmed at the Red Road flats in Glasgow, which when built in the 1960s were the highest residential blocks in Europe. The film has won eighteen awards including five BAFTAs.

2012: SKYFALL *directed by Sam Mendes*

The twenty-third Bond movie was filmed partly in Scotland, and the Glencoe scenes in particular made an impact – in 2014, NTS recorded an increase in visitors to the area of over forty per cent as a result of the film.

—— Six Great Screen Actors ——

FINLAY CURRIE (1878–1968)

A true Victorian, Currie was educated at George Watson's School in Edinburgh, and became a church organist and choirmaster. His first stage appearance was at the Edinburgh Pavilion in 1898, and his first movie (aged fifty-four) was *The Case of the Frightened Lady* (1932). His most famous role was as Magwitch in David Lean's film of *Great Expectations* (1946), but as George MacDonald Fraser pointed out, his frequent appearances as a white-haired prophetic figure in films such as *Quo Vadis* (1951) led generations of cinema-goers to imagine the end of the world as being heralded with a Scottish accent: 'Aye, weel…'

JIMMY FINLAYSON (1887–1953)

Born in Larbert, Finlayson attended George Watson's School in Edinburgh. He dropped out of Edinburgh University and won the lead in a West End play, *Bunty Pulls the Strings*, emigrating to New York in 1912 to play the role on Broadway. Finlayson drifted into the movies, and was one of the first Keystone Kops. He is most famous now for his roles in over thirty Laurel and Hardy films, and for his over-the-top double-takes, squint, and clearly false moustache. When sound came, his trade-mark exclamation was 'D'oh!' – to be borrowed later by Dan Castellaneta for Homer Simpson.

DEBORAH KERR (1921–2007)
Born in Helensburgh, Kerr was nominated six times for an Oscar. She never won, but was given a special award by the Motion Picture Academy in 1994 for her 'Perfection, Discipline and Elegance', which fairly sums up her film career, if you add 'Beauty and Wit'. MGM billed her as 'Kerr rhymes with Star!' Highlights include the extraordinary *Black Narcissus* (1947), *From Here to Eternity* (1953), with the famous wave-crashing beach scene with Burt Lancaster, *The King and I* (1956), and *The Innocents* (1961).

MOIRA SHEARER (1926–2006)
Born in Dunfermline, she was an acclaimed ballet dancer before making the film that propelled her into stardom, Powell and Pressburger's great ballet movie *The Red Shoes* (1948), a film in which her hair famously matched her shoes. Twelve years later Shearer played a murder victim in Powell's creepy thriller *Peeping Tom* (1960).

SEAN CONNERY (born 1930)
Formerly an Edinburgh milkman called 'Big Tam', Connery has made many fine movies from *The Hill* (1965) to *The Name of the Rose* (1986), but is of course forever identified with James Bond. He is quite possibly the most famous Scot in the world – and an ardent supporter of Scottish nationalism who has been a tax exile for many years.

EWAN MCGREGOR (born 1971)
Born in Perth, McGregor played the main character in *Train-spotting* and the young Obi-Wan Kenobi in the *Star Wars*

'prequel' trilogy. Versatile, talented, and fortunate, McGregor has become one of the leading movie actors of his generation. He is the nephew of Scots actor Denis Lawson, who played Wedge Antilles in the first *Star Wars* film.

—— Twelve Great TV Shows ——
(and *Outlander*)

1958–68: WHITE HEATHER CLUB

The BBC Scottish country dance show that defined Scotland for non-Scots, and brought tears to the eyes of Scots everywhere, though by the mid-sixties tears of embarrassment swamped the tears of joy. Clips can be found on the web. The show had at least one great musician, however, the accordionist Jimmy Shand (one of George Martin's favourite musicians), and some of the singers, such as Andy Stewart, were very good indeed. At its peak the show had an audience of 10 million. The great tenor Kenneth McKellar was also a frequent guest, though of course he never performed his spectacularly filthy version of 'The Ball of Kirriemuir' (yes, it's on YouTube).

1962–71: DR FINLAY'S CASEBOOK

Much loved and fondly remembered, the series was about a pre-NHS medical practice in the fictional toon of Tannoch-brae. Young Dr Finlay was the heart-throb, old Dr Cameron the wise mentor, and Janet was the housekeeper. Perhaps the most popular British TV show of the 1960s.

1964: CULLODEN

This remarkable (black and white) reconstruction of the Battle of Culloden is still regarded as one of the finest drama-documentaries produced by the BBC. The battle scenes are utterly convincing, and the cast were mostly local and amateur.

1965–74: THE VITAL SPARK

Stories of a Clyde puffer and its crew, based on the wonderful Para Handy stories by Neil Munro. A series was made in 1959 but nothing of that survives, or indeed of many later programmes. The BBC has issued a DVD with all the surviving episodes. Starring Roddy Macmillan and John Grieve, the series was very Scottish and very funny. A later (also excellent) series in 1995 starred Gregor Fisher.

1983–2010: TAGGART

Made by ITV, *Taggart* is the world's longest running police series; DCI Taggart himself was lost to the series in 1994, when the actor who played him, Mark McManus, died. Plots revolve around a fictional CID unit at the real Maryhill Police Station (it is claimed that Japanese tourists have been seen taking pictures of the station). Filmed in and around Glasgow, practically every actor with a Scots accent has appeared in it at one time or another. Essential quotes: 'Naebody move'; 'There's been a murrrder'; 'Erza boady in the close'.

1987: TUTTI FRUTTI

Another gem from BBC Scotland, written by John Byrne, this story of a band of old rockers, the Majestics, featured some future big names, including Robbie Coltrane, Emma Thompson, and Richard Wilson. It won six BAFTAs.

1988–99: RAB C. NESBITT

Seen by some as a marginally less offensive Scottish stereotype than the *White Heather Club*, the BBC's *Rab C. Nesbitt* sitcom – featuring Gregor Fisher as the feckless, unemployable Glaswegian Rab – began as a segment of the *Naked Video* sketch show in 1988 before shuffling out on its own. The dialogue crackled. On being told by a nurse that her stitches have burst,

Rab's wife Mary replies: 'Oh, thank goodness for that, nurse. For a minute there I thought I'd pissed masel.' The fine dialogue and rattling jokes tended to disguise the fact that much of what was happening in the Nesbitt life was actually as bleak as Rab's 'simmit', his unspeakable string vest. It was filmed mostly in Glasgow.

1992–6: MACHAIR

Perhaps not 'great' but certainly out of the ordinary, *Machair* was the first Scots Gaelic TV 'soap'. Shown on STV and filmed in the Gaelic-speaking heartland, the island of Lewis, it is fondly remembered by Gaels and non-Gaels. A 'machair' is a fertile raised beach found on Scottish islands: a pretty rare phenomenon with a unique ecosystem, much like the human population of Lewis.

1995–7: HAMISH MACBETH

From the novels by Marion Chesney, writing under the name of M. C. Beaton. A charming series depicting the adventures of a rather idle but problem-solving Highland cop who resists being promoted out of his comfy existence. Starred Robert Carlyle, assisted by a Westie called Wee Jock. Like Bill Forsyth's movies, the series was condemned by the Scottish arts police as whimsical and not serious. It was filmed near the palm trees of Plockton.

1999–2002: CHEWIN' THE FAT

A BBC sketch show written by Greg Hemphill and Ford Kiernan, who were also the leading performers. Some of the catchphrases have lingered in Scottish life, such as 'Gonnae no dae that?'

2002–5: BALAMORY

BBC children's show with regular characters and songs, filmed mostly in Glasgow and in and around Tobermory, Mull. It achieved huge success and is often parodied. The catchphrase 'What's the Story in Balamory?' seems likely to survive the show's surprising demise; apparently it came to an end because some of the cast wanted to move on. The show brought many tourists to Tobermory, where they were not universally welcomed ('all those kids running about' as one cheery local put it).

2002–2007: STILL GAME

A spin-off from *Chewin' the Fat*, *Still Game* stars Kiernan and Hemphill as two spirited old codgers, Jack and Victor, living in a deprived part of Glasgow. The show rapidly acquired a large UK following, and has a good ensemble of supporting actors, notably Sanjeev Kohli as the shopkeeper Navid Harrid. Like its parent show, *Still Game* is very funny, very witty, and with wee dark corners under the laughter.

2014–2016: OUTLANDER

Whatever one's view of the historical merits of the TV series *Outlander* (based on the novels by Diana Gabaldon), it has been phenomenally popular (on Netflix), and a lot of care has been taken to get some details right, e.g. the costumes. The story line is based on a Second World War nurse being transported back to 1743 through touching a stone circle that is also a time machine. Culloden is presented as an England–Scotland match. Doune Castle features as Castle Leoch, and consequently saw a rise of forty-four per cent in visitor numbers.

13

ENTERTAINERS AND MUSICIANS

❖

—— Eight Great Entertainers ——

SIR HARRY LAUDER (1870–1950)

Born in Portobello, Lauder became one of the high lords of the exhausting and often unforgiving worlds of British music hall and American Vaudeville. He first began as an 'Irish' comedian in the 1890s, but it was his Scottish act for which he became best known, appearing with kilt and a knobbly walking stick. In the early 1900s he was a big hit in London and took New York by storm in 1907. Ever versatile, Lauder was also very good in drag (photographs of the young Lauder dressed as a woman are disturbingly appealing), and he was enthusiastically received in Glasgow pantomimes. His songs, such as 'I Love a Lassie' and 'Roamin' in the Gloamin', were enormously popular. His son was killed in the First World War, and Lauder got his knighthood for fundraising work for the troops. He last appeared on stage in the Gorbals in 1947 at the age of seventy-seven, in a benefit for a scout troop.

DUNCAN MACRAE (1905–67)

Born in Glasgow, Macrae became a staple figure in films set in Scotland, from *Whisky Galore* in 1949 onwards. He was also the first televized Para Handy. For many Scots staring in boredom at Hogmanay TV 'specials' in the 1960s, Macrae was a lifesaver with his recitation of 'The Wee Cock Sparra'. He played Inspector Mathis in *Casino Royale*.

CHIC MURRAY *(1919–85)*

Regarded by many Scots as the funniest man who ever lived, you can see flashes of his unique style in *Gregory's Girl*. He once did an act with his wife billed as 'The Tall Droll with the Small Doll'. He belonged to the old variety tradition, but his comic view is also related to that of the strange world of Ivor Cutler. Two Chic Murray jokes: 'I had a tragic childhood. My parents never understood me. They were Japanese.' 'So I gave him a wave. Actually, it was more of a half wave, because I only half know him.'

IVOR CUTLER *(1923–2006)*

Being unclassifiable, the Glasgow-born Cutler was often called a 'Scottish surrealist'. He is best remembered for his appearance as Buster Bloodvessel in the Beatles' *Magical Mystery Tour* (1967), and for the monologues and songs from his *Life in a Scotch Sitting Room* album on John Peel's Radio 1 show (he was one of the very few artists of any kind to be a regular on both Radio 1 and Radio 3). When he died, a British tabloid printed the headline – 'Silly Poet Dies' – a headline he would undoubtedly have enjoyed.

RIKKI FULTON *(1924–2004)*

Glasgow-born, Fulton was one half (with Jack Milroy) of the double act Francie and Josie, two Glasgow wide boys, enormously popular on STV in the early 1960s. His comedy sketch show, *Scotch and Wry*, ran from the 1970s through the 1980s and became essential viewing for Scots – his lugubrious, drunken minister, the Reverend I. M. Jolly, was especially popular. Fulton played the KGB chief Pribluda in *Gorky Park*

(1983), which was filmed in Dundee; director Michael Apted cast him because he 'had never seen such cruel eyes'. Fulton served in the navy during the Second World War and was on HMS *Ibis* when she was torpedoed off Algiers in 1942; he was pushed away from a raft by panicking sailors and spent five hours in the water before being rescued. He later served on D-Day. His later years were clouded by Alzheimer's disease and he died after contracting MRSA in hospital.

STANLEY BAXTER *(born 1926)*
Like Billy Connolly, Baxter was not only a Glasgow-born genius of a comedian but also a highly influential one, demonstrating that comedy could be taken to different levels and still be immensely popular. His Christmas TV 'specials' in the 1970s were eagerly anticipated by all, but came to an end when the budgets began to shrivel; he refused to compromise and do them on the cheap. A gifted pantomine star and parodist, Baxter impersonated everyone from Noël Coward to Schnozzle Durante, and also the Pope and the Queen (very daring for the seventies). His skits on Glasgow patter on his 'Parliamo Glasgow' radio and TV sketches (and subsequent books) were also hugely popular.

BILLY CONNOLLY *(born 1942)*
The 'Big Yin' was born in Glasgow, and after school completed his apprenticeship at the shipyards as a welder (he also served as a Territorial in the Parachute Regiment). Connolly began performing as a folk singer (he is a fair hand at the banjo) and created what became known as 'alternative comedy' in the gaps between the songs. No topic was off-limits to Connolly, from God to flatulence. He had magnificently bad taste and revelled in it – so did the audiences. A new kind of stand-up comedy was born. Connolly has appeared in many

movies, including *Indecent Proposal* (1993), *Muppet Treasure Island* (1996), and *Mrs Brown* (1997). He was the patron of the Lonach Gathering Highland Games held in Strathdon, where he had a house (he is now mostly resident on the American West Coast). Connolly's early audiences got the impression that he was a Partick Thistle supporter but he later declared his undying love for Celtic. He is one of the few non-footballers to have taken part in a Celtic 'huddle'.

THE KRANKIES

The Krankies are a husband and wife team, Ian and Janette Tough (both born 1947): they play a father and his son, the father played by Jimmy Tough, and the son – 'Wee Jimmy Krankie' – by Janette. They began as a teenage act entertaining American troops and rose to fame as hosts of BBC TV show *Crackerjack* in the 1980s, becoming established pantomine artistes along the way (they also had three TV series). They made a memorable appearance in a French and Saunders spoof of *The Silence of the Lambs*, and have also been in the *Beano*. Their catchprase is 'Fandabidozi'.

—— A Few Folkies and Trads ——

ALLY BAIN (born 1946)

Fiddle music is fundamental to Scottish folk music, and Shetlander Ally Bain is the modern master of the Scots fiddle as well as being a noted historian of British fiddle traditions.

CAPERCAILLIE

Gaelic folk band featuring the fine singer Karen Matheson (she has a cameo in *Rob Roy*).

The Corries

Originally a folk trio, the Corries became best known in the 1960s as the duo of Roy Williamson (1936–90) and Ronnie Browne. Williamson wrote their best-known song, 'Flower of Scotland', a celebration of the Scottish victory at Bannockburn, a song that is, depending on your point of view, either a moving celebration of Scottish national pride or a god-awful dirge. It was first adopted by rugby fans in the 1970s as an unofficial national anthem for the Scotland team.

Dick Gaughan (born 1948)

Folk singer, songwriter, and socialist, Gaughan has collaborated with many other like-minded musicians, such as Boys of the Lough, and formed Clan Alba in 1991.

Jean Redpath (born 1937)

Born in Edinburgh, Redpath is one of the greatest interpreters of Scottish song. She is most famous as a singer of Burns lyrics and traditional songs.

Jimmy Shand (1908–2000)

Born in Fife and brought up in Auchtermuchty, like many another Fife lad, Shand went down the pit at the age of fourteen. His musical career took off after the Second World War and he had a Top 20 hit in 1955 with 'The Bluebell Polka' (produced by George Martin and available on George Martin's *Highlights from 50 Years in Recording* CD), and was a regular presence on the *White Heather Club* with Andy Stewart. From the 1970s onwards Shand's reputation grew to the point where he is now regarded as having been one of Scotland's few world-class musicians. He was given an MBE in 1962 and became Sir James Shand in 1999.

THE SINGING KETTLE *(founded mid-1980s)*

The Singing Kettle is an extraordinarily successful children's group, founded by husband and wife team Cilla Fisher and Artie Trezise. The group sings traditional Scottish songs adapted for children and has grown from performing in nurseries to becoming a huge draw (one of the biggest in Scotland) with a worldwide fan base. Besides being great fun, the group has done much to keep Scottish folk music alive and interesting to children. All together now: 'Spout, handle, lid of metal, What's inside the Singing Kettle?'

ANDY STEWART *(1933–93)*

Andy Stewart compered the *White Heather Club* in the 1960s and had several hits in the UK with songs such as 'A Scottish Soldier' (1961). Stewart was a very fine singer. His recording of 'Donald, Where's Yer Troosers?' includes an impression of Elvis that reputedly impressed the King himself.

—— Bagpipe Music ——

Like haggis, bagpipes belong to many cultures but are now most closely identified with Scotland, and the form of bagpipe most people now think of when the instrument is mentioned is the 'Great Highland Bagpipe', that of the pipe bands. Tunes for the pipes range from laments to war music – the instrument is unmatched for both – and also to dance music. Boswell described dancing to the bagpipe on Skye thus: 'We danced to night to the musick of the bagpipe, which made us beat the ground with prodigious force.' (Dr Johnson loved the pipes and would press his ear against them to hear the music better.) The tunes are called pibrochs and are either *ceòl mòr*, the 'great music' of war or commemoration, or *ceòl beag*, the 'small music' of reels and dances.

According to Skye tradition, the MacCrimmons, hereditary pipers to the MacLeod chiefs, were the greatest of all pipers, and ran a piping school at Boreraig (at which women also played).

—— Twenty-five Musicians and Bands ——

This section is arranged alphabetically by band name or artist and could have gone on for a long time, which is why it has an arbitrary limit of twenty-five: it does *not* represent a 'top' list of any kind, but is rather a wee briefing on the huge variety of Scottish rock and pop talent.

SUSAN BOYLE *(born 1961)*
Scottish chanteuse who became a sensation after appearing on the TV reality show *Britain's Got Talent* in 2009. Her first album acheived record international sales.

JACK BRUCE *(born 1943)*
Bassist and vocalist for iconic rock band Cream; the other members were Eric Clapton and Ginger Baker.

DAVID BYRNE *(born 1952)*
Dumbarton-born musician who founded Talking Heads, Byrne has worked in all forms of media; his collaborators include Bowie and Eno.

DONOVAN *(born Donovan Leitch in Glasgow, 1946)*
Folk/pop singer and hippie icon who has stayed true to the Maharishi tradition. His hits include 'Mellow Yellow'.

BILL DRUMMOND *(born 1953)*
Co-founder of the KLF (or the Justified Ancients of Mu Mu),

a 1980s acid house band (among other things). He is the only Scot known to have ritually burned £1 million – on Jura.

SHEENA EASTON *(born 1959)*
Has impeccable working-class credentials (dad was a steel-worker), won two Grammys, has sold over 4 million albums, sang a James Bond theme ('For Your Eyes Only'), has appeared in several movies and TV shows (including five episodes of *Miami Vice*), and is therefore not rated in Scotland.

FRANZ FERDINAND
Band formed in Glasgow in 2000 and became huge very quickly. Alex Kapranos is lead vocalist. Hits include 'Take Me Out'.

FISH *(born Derek Dick, 1958)*
Former member of Marillion, now frequently classified as a 'prog rocker'. His fans are called 'Fishheads' (the name 'Fish' supposedly originated from his fondness for baths).

ELIZABETH FRASER *(born 1963)*
Singer with the Cocteau Twins and This Mortal Coil. Her best known song is probably her haunting version of Tim Buckley's 'Song to the Siren'. She can be heard on the soundtracks of *The Lord of the Rings* movies.

ALEX HARVEY *(1935–82)*
His Sensational Alex Harvey Band was popular in the 1970s. Still classed in pop history as a glam rock outfit, but Harvey led the band into strange musical places.

BERT JANSCH *(born 1943)*
Singer/songwriter, founder member of Pentangle in 1968. One of the most influential guitarists of the 1960s.

Mark Knopfler (born 1948)

Born in Glasgow to a Hungarian–Jewish father and an English mother, therefore a typical Scot. Co-founder of Dire Straits in 1977; a massively influential figure as a guitarist, Knopfler is also a highly rated record producer and has written film scores, including *Local Hero*.

Annie Lennox (born 1954)

Aberdeen-born singer-songwriter and lead singer (1980–90, 1999–present) of Eurythmics. Lennox was once voted 'the greatest white soul singer alive'.

Lulu (born Marie Lawrie in Glasgow, 1948)

Lulu had her first hit record in 1964 aged fifteen: 'Shout'. Her singing/acting career (she is a gifted comic actress) has now lasted for over forty years.

Rose McDowall (born 1959)

One half, with Jill Bryson, of Strawberry Switchblade, Glasgow's main contribution to the art-punk/goth scene: they had a 1984 hit with 'Since Yesterday'. The pair disbanded in 1986, and McDowall went on to sing solo and with various other outfits such as Death in June. One of Scotland's many lovely voices.

Billy Mackenzie (1957–97)

Dundee-born lead singer of the Associates, a new wave eighties band. Mackenzie, who became an influential figure, had a wide vocal range and theatrical stage manner. Morrissey's song 'William, It Was Really Nothing' was supposedly about Mackenzie, who suffered from depression and killed himself.

NAZARETH

Heavy rock band founded in Dunfermline in 1968, and have continued into the noughties (but have still not been in the business as long as Lulu). Their hits include a justly famous cover version of Joni Mitchell's 'This Flight Tonight'.

THE PROCLAIMERS (born 1962)

The Auchtermuchty-bred, identical twins Craig and Charlie Reid. Great songwriters: 'Letter from America' and 'I'm Gonna Be (500 Miles)' are modern classics. They are nationalists, socialists, and devoted Hibs supporters: their 'Sunshine on Leith' has become a club anthem.

ANNIE ROSS (born 1930)

Jazz singer and member of the trio Lambert, Hendricks, and Ross, 1957–62. Ross is regarded as one of the finest jazz singers. She is supposed to have dubbed Britt Ekland's singing voice in *The Wicker Man*, but this is disputed. She is the sister of the entertainer and impresario Jimmy Logan (died 2001).

RUNRIG

Skye-based folk-rock band founded in 1973: singer Donnie Munro joined in 1974, leaving in 1997 to pursue a career in politics on behalf of the Labour Party. Another ex-Runrig member, Pete Wishart, became SNP MP for Perth and North Perthshire and is said to be the only MP who has previously played on *Top of the Pops*.

TEXAS

Glasgow rock band founded in 1988; the name is taken from the Wim Wenders movie *Paris, Texas* (Glasgow bands have a reputation for being pretentious). The lead singer, Sharleen

Spiteri, is widely recognized as having one of the great rock voices, female or male.

K T Tunstall (born Kate Tunstall in Edinburgh, 1975)
Adopted eighteen days after her birth, the Scottish singer-songwriter Tunstall has a huge following all over the world. Her song 'Suddenly I See' was used by Hillary Clinton as her campaign theme song at Democratic presidential nomination rallies in 2008. Tunstall herself, however, declared her support for Obama because of her opposition to the Iraq War.

Midge Ure (born 1953)
Born in Cambuslang, Ure was a member of the band Ultravox in the 1980s. In 1984 he wrote (with Bob Geldof) the Band Aid single 'Do They Know It's Christmas?', helped organize Live Aid that year, and also Live 8 in 2005.

Wet Wet Wet
Founded in 1982 in Clydebank as Vortex Motion, the Wets were a highly successful 1980s band fronted by Marti Pellow. Their best known hit single, 'Love is All Around', became one of the most annoying sounds of the nineties.

Lena Zavaroni (1963–99)
Born in Rothesay to an Italian-Scottish family, Zavaroni won *Opportunity Knocks* for five weeks running in 1974. She is apparently the youngest person (aged ten) to have had an album in the UK top ten – *Ma! He's Making Eyes at Me* – and performed in Hollywood with Sinatra. She died as a result of anorexia.

The Scottish landscape and literary traditions have inspired much notable music, from Mendelssohn's *Hebrides Overture* (or *Fingal's Cave*) to Beethoven's setting of Scottish lyrics, but Scotland also produced – and still produces – great classical music.

ROBERT CARVER (c.1487–c.1568)

Carver was probably born in Aberdeen of uncertain parentage: we don't even know for certain what his real name was. He became a monk at Scone Abbey, and adopted the pseudonym Robert Arnot. Biographers are rightly cautious about the details of Carver's life: whoever he was, he was a marvellous composer, one of Europe's finest from the sixteenth-century Renaissance.

All his surviving works – five masses and two motets – are in a precious manuscript called the Carver Choirbook (formerly the Scone Antiphonary) held in the National Library of Scotland. His works are regularly performed and there are several fine recordings.

THOMAS ERSKINE, 6TH EARL OF KELLIE (1732–81)

Kellie (who was usually called Kelly) was born at Kellie Castle in Fife, to a Jacobite family. He was a member of the Edinburgh Musical Society in his late teens and in 1753 was in Europe, studying the violin at Mannheim. His father died in 1756 and he returned to Scotland, selling all the family property except for the castle. Kellie was a senior Freemason, a member of the Highland Society in London, and a serious drinker: the actor Samuel Foote suggested his red face could ripen cucumbers. He had ten symphonies published in the 1760s and composed songs and chamber music. Not much of his music survives, but enough for the *New Grove* to call him 'arguably Scotland's greatest classical composer'. A collection of his chamber music was discovered in 1971.

WILLIAM MARSHALL (1748–1833)

Born in Fochabers, Marshall was an excellent violinist and was described by Burns as 'the first [i.e. best] composer of strathspeys of the age'. Marshall can be seen as both a folk artist – a master of the traditional styles of fiddle playing – and as a master of the Scottish baroque. The modern label of 'cross-over' is applicable to his output. His reels and strathspeys are still popular. He was also a renowned clock maker, and at least three of his clocks survive.

ALEXANDER MACKENZIE (1847–1935)

Mackenzie's father was an Edinburgh composer and violin-ist, who sent the boy to Germany to study music, where he too became a violinist. He became precentor of St George's Church, Edinburgh, in 1870, and began composing canta-tas, oratorios, and operas. Mackenzie also composed a comic opera in the style of Gilbert and Sullivan, *His Majesty* (1897). Two of his most popular works are the *Violin Concerto* (1885) and the *Pibroch Suite* (1889).

HAMISH MACCUNN (1868–1916)

MacCunn was born in Greenock, the son of a shipowner, and became one of Scotland's leading exponents of Roman-tic music. He studied at the Royal College of Music under Sir Hubert Parry. His first overture, *Cior Mhor* (1885), was described by George Bernard Shaw as 'a charming Scotch overture that carries you over the hill and far away'. MacCunn's best known work is *The Land of the Mountain and the Flood* (1885), a fine atmospheric composition. He also wrote two operas: *Jeanie Deans* (1894) and *Diarmid* (1897).

THEA MUSGRAVE *(born 1928)*

Born in Edinburgh, Musgrave became one of the leading composers of her generation and one of the very few to be female: 'Yes, I am a woman, and I am a composer,' she has said. An a cappella work of hers was performed at the 2006 BBC Proms – she was, at the age of seventy-eight, the only woman out of 106 composers featured (Anne Philidor being male). She also conducts her own works sometimes, for example the ballet *Beauty and the Beast* (1969) and the opera *Mary, Queen of Scots* (1977).

RONALD STEVENSON *(born 1928)*

Stevenson was born in Blackburn. His father was Scots and he moved to Scotland in the mid-1950s, so we can claim him. He is a prolific composer: he has written song cycles, much keyboard music, chamber and choral music, and works for orchestra, including *Jamboree for Grainger* (1960–1) and *Young Scotland Suite* (1976).

CRAIG ARMSTRONG *(born 1955)*

Most Scots have never heard of Craig Armstrong but we have all heard his music since he began writing for the screen. Films for which Armstrong has written music include *Moulin Rouge* (2001), *Love, Actually* (2003), and *Elizabeth: The Golden Age* (2007). He has also worked with many pop acts, including U2 and Madonna.

JAMES MACMILLAN *(born 1959)*

MacMillan was born in Kilwinning, Ayrshire. His first major work was *The Confession of Isobel Gowdie* (1990). Gowdie had been accused of witchcraft in 1662, and the composition, says MacMillan, 'craves absolution and offers Isobel Gowdie the mercy and humanity that was denied her in the last days of her life'. The work was an immediate success, establishing MacMillan as an important new voice. MacMillan is a Roman Catholic and his strong concern with social justice is linked to his religious views, and to his music. Other works include *Veni, Veni, Emmanuel* (1992), a percussion concerto for Evelyn Glennie, the opera *Inés de Castro* (1996), and *From Ayrshire*, a violin piece for the brilliant young Scottish violinist Nicola Benedetti. MacMillan has been an outspoken critic of sectarianism in Scotland, and once described Scotland as often 'inward-looking' and 'xenophobic'.

DAME EVELYN GLENNIE *(born 1965)*

Glennie was brought up on an Aberdeenshire farm, and has been deaf since the age of twelve. She is regarded as one of the world's leading percussionists and was awarded a DBE in the 2007 New Year's Honours list. A gifted composer, she has collaborated with many other artists, including Bjork and Ray Davies, and did the music for a Mazda advert.

14

ART AND ARCHITECTURE

❖

ART

—— Five Iconic Paintings ——

THE REVEREND ROBERT WALKER SKATING ON
DUDDINGSTON LOCH *(1790s) by Sir Henry Raeburn
(1756–1823), in the National Gallery of Scotland, Edinburgh*
This is one of Scotland's best loved paintings – and a good
earner for the National Gallery in reproduction fees. The Reverend
Walker (1716–83) was minister at the Canongate Kirk,
and was noted for his generosity. The picture is unsigned, and
in 2005 an attribution controversy arose: it was suggested
that the painting is not by Raeburn, but by the French artist
Henri-Pierre Danloux. The debate continues but the consensus
seems to be that it is in fact a Raeburn painting.

ALEXANDER RANALDSON MACDONELL OF
GLENGARRY *(1812) by Sir Henry Raeburn (1756–1823),
in the National Gallery of Scotland, Edinburgh*
Macdonell's Gaelic nickname was Alasdair Fiadhaich ('Fierce
Alasdair'), and he was indeed an irascible character who once
killed a fellow officer in a duel at Fort George in 1798. He was
the 15th chief of his clan, and was not a popular man: contemporaries
remarked on his arrogance and pride, qualities
his acquaintance Sir Walter Scott humanized when using him

as a model for the character of MacIvor in *Waverley* (1814). Raeburn's portrait of the man shows Macdonell as he saw himself: the noble Celtic warrior and aristocrat, a stereotype that endures. The image does not fit the reality: in 1807 a court found him guilty of assaulting a tenant, and questioned his fitness to hold office – he was a JP and deputy lord lieutenant at the time. Macdonell raised a regiment by threatening to evict the families of tenants who refused to sign up, and happily cleared large numbers of his tenants for sheep farming.

THE MONARCH OF THE GLEN *(1851) by Sir Edwin Landseer (1802–73), in the Diageo Collection*

London-born Landseer loved the Highlands and liked painting animals – his works include the lion sculptures below Nelson's Column. Gruesome things, however, often happened to animals in his work, such as the startlingly violent *The Swannery Invaded by Sea Eagles* (1869). This stag gets off lightly, and was painted for the House of Lords, which reneged on its promise to buy it. The painting was sold to Pears Soap, and was then sold on to the Dewar distillery. *The Monarch of the Glen* has become one of the defining images of Scotland.

THE LAST OF THE CLAN *(1865) by Thomas Faed (1826– 1900), in Kelvingrove Art Gallery and Museum, Glasgow*

The painting depicts an old clan chief with the few remnants of the clan: a couple of young women and children staring out to sea as the rope that holds the ship to the shore is cast off, and the young men of the clan depart. Once dismissed in the early twentieth century as an example of Victorian sentimentalism, modern viewers see this great painting again as the Victorians saw it at its exhibition at the Royal Academy in London, as a moving depiction of loss, and of forced exile.

CHRIST OF ST JOHN OF THE CROSS *(1951) by*
Salvador Dali (1904–89), in Kelvingrove Art Gallery and
Museum, Glasgow

Not a Scottish painter, nor a Scottish subject, but Dali's great painting has become part of the cultural fabric of Glasgow since a wise director of Glasgow Museums, Dr Honeyman, persuaded the city fathers to release the money to buy the work in 1952. The price of £8,200 (soon recouped from reproduction fees) was met from the remnants of the profits from the 1901 Kelvingrove International Exhibition, so the painting actually cost Glasgow Council nothing (except humble gratitude to both Dr Honeyman and the Victorian city fathers).

—— The Glasgow Boys ——

The designation 'Glasgow Boys' was adopted by a group of young artists who flourished from the 1870s up to the 1890s. There were about twenty of them, most from Glasgow, one (Joseph Crawhall) from England and even a few from Edinburgh. The Glasgow Boys liked Whistler and the new style of French naturalism, and disliked the commonplace 'genre' painting of the day; they also disliked Edinburgh's dominance in Scottish art. *The Dictionary of National Biography* describes them as 'a coherent force in Scottish painting', which they were, but they were also quite disparate. Three representative figures are:

SIR JOHN LAVERY *(1856–1941)*

Born in Belfast, Lavery was apprenticed to a Glasgow photographer, but instead decided he was a painter. The *Dictionary of National Biography* gives instances of his notable ruthlessness: the abandonment of his pregnant unmarried sister (who drowned herself in the Clyde), and a mysterious fire that destroyed his studio shortly after he insured it. One of the most remarkable works of this unlovely man is *The State Visit of Queen Victoria to the International Exhibition, Glasgow, 1888*, which combines 253 portraits (Victoria gave him a twenty-minute sitting). He used his wife, Hazel Lavery, as the model for the portrait of Ireland's personification, Cathleen ni Houlihan, used on Free State banknotes.

Sir James Guthrie (1859–1930)
Born in Greenock, his Courbet-like *A Funeral Service in the Highlands* (1882) sums up the Glasgow Boys' aspirations. Guthrie later became a very successful portraitist.

Edward Hornel (1864–1933)
Hornel was born in the improbably named Bacchus Marsh, Australia. The family were from Kirkcudbright; they returned there in 1866, and the town became Hornel's home for the rest of his long life. Hornel's subjects include Druids and goblins and he developed a great interest in Japanese art. His painting was a conscious attempt to move away from the Glasgow Boys framework, and is so unrealistic and vibrant that Liverpool City Councillors complained when it was bought for the city's Walker Art Gallery. Hornel was idiosyncratic and very much his own man.

By 1891, there were strange new growths in Scottish art…

—— The Glasgow Girls and —— the Glasgow School

The 1890s were a time of innovation in Western art, but one thing about the age that is undeservedly forgotten is the highly unusual (for anywhere) coalescence of women artists, designers and illustrators that came about in the west of Scotland. The high point of this movement was 1890–1910, and the group was dubbed the 'Glasgow Girls' in a conscious echo of the Glasgow Boys. The 'Girls' were part of a wider movement called the Glasgow Style, a form of Art Nouveau. The Glasgow Girls included the designer **Jessie Newberry**, the book illustrator **Jessie M. King**, and the sisters **Frances and Margaret MacDonald**. Margaret married Charles Rennie Mackintosh and in 2008 her panel *The White Rose and the Red Rose* set a world auction record for a Scottish work of art, fetching £1.7 million.

—— The Scottish Colourists ——

The group of four artists known as the Scottish Colourists flourished in the 1920s and 1930s. The group acquired its collective name as a result of a shared interest in the vivid colours in French post-Impressionist art. Monet, Matisse and Cézanne were notable influences.

SAMUEL PEPLOE (1871–1935)
Edinburgh-born Peploe studied art in Paris where he met Fergusson, who like himself was fascinated by Whistler, the Glasgow Boys and post-Impressionism. He later met Cadell, with whom he was to share a love of Iona, and is especially noted for his landscapes and still lifes. A painting that may or may not be by Peploe features in Alexander McCall Smith's novel *44 Scotland Street* (2004).

JOHN DUNCAN FERGUSSON (1874–1961)
Born in Leith, Fergusson studied art in Edinburgh in the early 1890s, and was influenced by the Glasgow Boys. By the time he moved to France in 1913, Fergusson was an established artist

and he became much influenced by fauvism. He returned to Britain in 1914, and married the dancer Margaret Morris in 1918.

LESLIE HUNTER (1877–1931)

Hunter was born in Rothesay, and moved to California with his family in 1892, where he learned to paint. He returned to Scotland between 1903 and 1905 and visited Paris, but, annoyingly, it is not known if he came across the (regularly exhibited) work of Fergusson and Peploe. He went back to San Francisco in 1905, where his work was destroyed in the 1906 earthquake, after which he moved to Glasgow. In 1916 Hunter exhibited with the Glasgow dealer Alexander Reid (who also exhibited van Gogh), and later met Fergusson and Peploe in the 1920s. His landscapes of Fife (and also of France) are reckoned to be his finest.

FRANCIS CADELL (1883–1937)

Born in Edinburgh, he studied in France, where he discovered Matisse, his greatest influence. He worked in oil and watercolour, and produced still lifes, landscapes, and highly regarded portraits such as *The Black Hat* (1914). He served in the First World War with the Royal Scots and the Argyll and Sutherland Highlanders. Cadell made several trips to Iona – which has light as magical as anywhere in France – with Peploe.

—— Four Great Photographers ——

People argue endlessly about whether or not photography is 'art': the Victorians seem to have been fairly sure that photography is indeed an art form, and four of the greatest names in the history of photography are the Scottish Victorians below.

DAVID OCTAVIUS HILL (1802–70) and ROBERT ADAMSON (1821–46)

Louis Daguerre proclaimed his photographic process in 1839; four years later, Robert Adamson opened his photographic studio in Calton Hill, Edinburgh. Adamson was an engineer (who died at the age of twenty-five, three years after opening the studio); Hill was a painter. The combination of art and science is oddly prescient for the future of photography, and, remarkably, Hill and Adamson's portraits, such as their photographs of Newhaven fisherfolk, are still regarded as masterworks.

JULIA MARGARET CAMERON (1815–79)

At forty-eight, Cameron took to the young art of photography late on, after her daughter had given her a camera as a present, but so mastered the discipline that she became one of the most noted portraitists of all time. In sixteen years she created an astonishing portfolio of work: the collection of portraits in particular, from her friend Tennyson to Garibaldi, became a portrait of the age.

ALEXANDER GARDNER (1821–82)

Born in Paisley, Gardner was, like many locals, an apprentice weaver and became a socialist. He emigrated to the US in 1856 and joined Matthew Brady's photographic business. Gardner quickly established himself as a great portrait photographer, and took many of the iconic images of the day – especially those of the Civil War.

ARCHITECTURE

Scottish architecture begins in prehistory with a unique form of architecture: the broch, from which many textbooks jump straight to Scottish baronial as the other notable form of native architecture, but there is much more…

—— Fifteen Castles ——

Castle Stalker

Like Eilean Donan, Castle Stalker is ridiculously picturesque on its tidal islet near Port Appin: unlike Eilean Donan and some other castles, however, Castle Stalker is absolutely for real: a medieval castle that has survived in much the same form since the mid-fifteenth century. It stars as Castle Aargh in *Monty Python and the Holy Grail* (1975).

Cawdor Castle

Between Inverness and Forres, Cawdor Castle is famous because of the Macbeth connection, but is remarkable in its own right. Beautiful, romantic, and well maintained, its construction began in the late fourteenth century.

Dunscaith Castle

An evocative ruin dating back to the fourteenth century on the Sleat Peninsula of Skye. A MacDonald castle, it was captured and retaken several times in the fourteenth and fifteenth centuries, and abandoned by the MacDonalds in the early seventeenth century. Legend tells us that the Irish hero Cuchulainn came here to learn sword fighting from Skye's warrior queen Sgathach, who supposedly gave her name to the original fort.

Dunvegan Castle

A magnificent Skye castle, one of the finest in Scotland. Home to the MacLeod of MacLeod, and occupied by the MacLeod family for around eight centuries, it is possibly the oldest continuously inhabited castle in Scotland. It contains many relics, among them the legendary Fairy Flag.

EDINBURGH CASTLE
Sited on top of an extinct volcano, where there have been fortifications since prehistory, the castle is Scotland's most popular tourist attraction. Its many treasures include the Scottish Crown Jewels, the Stone of Destiny, and the twelfth-century St Margaret's Chapel. Unmatched anywhere in the world.

EILEAN DONAN CASTLE
The small island of Donan is very picturesquely sited by Dornie, on the road to Skye. The first castle here was built in the thirteenth century, adapted over the centuries, and destroyed by bombardment in 1719; practically all of what you see today is an early twentieth-century reconstruction. Reputedly one of the most photographed rural castles in the world, it looks good from any angle and has featured in many films.

ELCHO CASTLE
Four miles from Perth, this fine castle dates from about 1570. Formerly home to the Wemyss family, the castle has been kept in very good condition. In a wonderful setting, it has a lovely garden; unlike many Scottish castles, this one is visitor-friendly.

GLAMIS CASTLE
Built in beautiful Strathmore by the village of Glamis, and inhabited by the same family for over 600 years, Glamis is the family home of the late Queen Mother, and the birthplace of Princess Margaret.

HERMITAGE CASTLE

Dating from the end of the fourteenth century, Hermitage is arguably the darkest and most forbidding castle in the world. Other castles – even when they clearly meant business – contrive to look attractive, but Hermitage is first and last a house of war. It stands at the head of Liddesdale Valley, in the Debatable Land fought over by England, Scotland, and every freebooting family in the Borders. Liddesdale and its dark lords (see p. 229) feature in many a Border ballad:

> Now Liddesdale has ridden a raid,
> But I wat they had better hae staid at hame,
> For Michael o' Winfield he is dead,
> And Jock o' the Side is prisoner ta'en.

HUNTINGTOWER CASTLE

Just west of Perth, Huntingtower was built by the Ruthven family in the fifteenth century. It's a somewhat unusual castle, consisting of two conjoined towers. Mary, Queen of Scots, and Darnley came here on their honeymoon.

INVERARAY CASTLE

A gloriously over-the-top multi-turreted castle, enclosed by four towers, Inveraray is the home of the Campbell family, whose chief is also the Duke of Argyll. The castle was designed by Sir John Vanbrugh and completed in 1789.

INVERGARRY CASTLE

Brooding on the Raven's Rock over Loch Oich in the Great Glen, Invergarry Castle was the seat of the MacDonnells of Glengarry and Clan Donald. The present castle dates from the seventeenth century. It was burned by government troops in 1746 and is in much need of restoration.

KISIMUL CASTLE

Kisimul Castle dominates Castle Bay on Barra and is exactly what it looks like: a stronghold for raiders. Kisimul is the castle of the MacNeils of Barra and the earliest parts may date from the eleventh century, but most of what you see was built in the fifteenth and sixteenth centuries. The old song 'Kishmul's Galley' celebrates the 'heroes' who manned the galleys, but the reality of the pirate trade driven from this castle was one of pillage, murder, rape, and children sold into slavery. The Kisimul galleys raided as far south as Bristol, well into Elizabeth I's reign. Elizabeth complained to James VI, but the galleys were still active after James inherited Elizabeth's throne.

STIRLING CASTLE

Sited, like Edinburgh Castle, on an extinct volcano, the magnificent Stirling Castle dominates the land for miles around. Most of the castle dates from the fifteenth and sixteenth centuries, though there are some earlier parts. (Edward I captured this formidable castle in 1304 with the aid of a massive siege engine called a Warwolf which threw huge missiles at the castle walls.)

URQUHART CASTLE

Urquhart Castle has a most romantic but also strategic setting overlooking Loch Ness: the waters around it plunge to a depth of 600 feet. A ruin now, the castle and its predecessors have been the focus of much conflict down the centuries. The last major damage was done in 1689, when a retreating Williamite garrison blew up most of the castle, after beating off a large Jacobite force.

—— Peel Towers ——

These structures can be seen on both sides of the Anglo-Scottish border, silent testimony to centuries of strife. A peel (or pele) tower served as an early warning system to detect Border reivers, and was also a refuge when the raiders arrived. The towers were not designed to hold out against armies, but could usually be held against horsemen in a hurry. A notable example is Smailholm Tower, an impressive keep built around the end of the fifteenth century, near Kelso; once owned by the Pringles, it passed to the Scotts. It is the setting for Sir Walter Scott's ballad 'The Eve of St John', and is referred to in 'Marmion':

> Then rise those crags, that mountain tower,
> Which charmed my fancy's wakening hour.

—— Ten Great Religious Buildings ——

DRYBURGH ABBEY
The monks who founded Dryburgh around 1150 wore white robes, like late period Gandalf, and it is easy to imagine what the abbey would have been like (much of the domestic detail survives) in its heyday. The abbey sits in beautiful seclusion, surrounded on three sides by the Tweed, but suffered badly during the Anglo–Scottish wars. One retreating English army burned it down because they were offended by the sound of its celebratory bells. Other great abbeys nearby are Kelso Abbey (founded 1128), Jedburgh Abbey (founded 1138), and Melrose Abbey (founded 1136).

DUNFERMLINE ABBEY
The Christian settlement at Dunfermline goes back to about 800. Benedictines were invited to start a priory church here

in 1072 by Malcolm III and his sainted wife Margaret. The abbey itself was founded by David I in 1128, who is buried here along with many other Scottish royals. Much of the old Norman abbey survives, despite assaults from Edward I and Protestant zealots.

GLASGOW CATHEDRAL
This magnificent cathedral was raised over Kentigern's c.550 settlement, and finally consecrated in 1197. The cathedral is by far the best preserved of the larger Scottish churches to have survived the Reformation, as the local masons and allied trades rallied to protect it. Rising above the cathedral is the fabulous Victorian Necropolis, with its many fine gravestones and monuments: on a quiet day, you may see deer here.

IONA ABBEY
Columba landed on Iona in 563 and used it as a base for spreading Christianity into Pictland. The abbey was sacked several times by Vikings, and was restored in the twentieth century. Some of the monuments here go back to the seventh century, and many kings of Scotland, Norway, and Ireland are believed to be buried here. Iona is a magical place, and Dr Johnson's words cannot be improved upon: 'That man is little to be envied, whose patriotism would not gain force upon the plain of Marathon, or whose piety would not grow warmer among the ruins of Iona!'

MELROSE ABBEY
Another great Border abbey, Melrose was founded by Cistercian monks in 1136 (at the request of King David I). The English king, Richard II, in a rare example of medieval Christian solidarity, gave it a grant in 1389 to show his regret for burning it in 1385.

ROSSLYN CHAPEL

At Roslin village, just outside Edinburgh, the chapel was founded by Sir William St Clair in 1446 and recently made famous by the *da Vinci Code* phenomenon. Rosslyn has always been recognized as a special place: the eighteenth-century antiquary John Britton praised its 'antiquity and eccentricity'. The interior suffered badly in the Reformation but many wonders remain, including the amazing roof and the Apprentice Pillar.

ST ANDREWS CATHEDRAL

Basically a set of ruins, but one of the greatest set of ruins in Europe. The cathedral was consecrated in 1318 in the presence of Robert the Bruce. It was subsequently attacked by both the English (who once stripped the lead off the roof) and the weather (a mighty wind blew down a wall), but it was the Reformation that did the real damage. After John Knox preached a sermon in St Andrews in 1559, a righteous mob stormed the cathedral destroying what they could of its interior, the first of a wave of Taliban attacks that left the ruin we have today.

ST GILES CATHEDRAL

Although commonly described as a cathedral, the High Kirk of St Giles was actually only a bishop's seat for 23 out of its 1,000 years of existence. Dedicated in 1243, substantially altered in the fifteenth century, and restored again in the nineteenth century, St Giles – with its prime Edinburgh location on the Royal Mile – is simply soaked in Scottish history. It is regarded as the mother church of world Presbyterianism.

ST MAGNUS CATHEDRAL

This is the most northerly cathedral in Britain and one of the most beautiful. It is on Viking land but of Norman construction, and must be one of the few cathedrals anywhere to have its own dungeon. After the canonization of Magnus in 1135, work on the cathedral dedicated to him began in 1137 (and may have been carried out by the same masons who built Durham Cathedral).

St Margaret's Church
In Restalrig Road, Edinburgh, this is a very fine example of an evolving Scottish church. A sixth-century saint, Triduana, is said to be buried here. There are ancient tombstones, Templar connections going back to the twelfth century, and an unusual fifteenth-century well and chapel. Substantially destroyed during the Reformation, the church was rebuilt in the Scottish baronial style in the nineteenth century.

—— A Spiritual Garden ——

The poet Ian Hamilton Finlay (1925–2006) first came to prominence as a writer of 'concrete' poetry, and began inscribing poems in concrete in a garden in the mid-sixties.

Strathclyde Regional Council refused to accept Finlay's definition of his garden as a temple. In 1983 Strathclyde officials tried to remove works from the garden in lieu of rates the region claimed were owed and were physically resisted by Finlay's supporters. The garden – at Dunsyre in Lanarkshire – was renamed Little Sparta, and was described by Sir Roy Strong as 'the only really original garden made in this country since 1945'. In 2004 Little Sparta was voted by a panel of fifty arts professionals as the most important work of Scottish art. The garden can be visited from June to September and is maintained by the Little Sparta Trust.

WILLIAM ADAM (1689–1748)

Regarded in the eighteenth and nineteenth centuries as Scotland's premier architect (and once described as Scotland's 'Universal Architect'), Adam's buildings include the superb renovation of Hopetoun House near Edinburgh, and Duff House in Banff. He began the building of Inveraray Castle in 1746.

ROBERT ADAM (1728–92)

Son of William Adam, and now considered to be a much greater architect. He was one of the leading neoclassical architects of his day, an architect worthy of the era of the Scottish Enlightenment. Adam's buildings include Culzean Castle (Ayrshire), Kedleston Hall (Derbyshire), and Pulteney Bridge (Bath). His brothers James (1732–94) and John (1721–92) were also noted architects.

DAVID BRYCE (1803–76)

Bryce developed and is the recognized master of the Scottish baronial style of architecture, a Gothic-revival style in which (mostly country) houses were decorated by turrets, towers, and crenellations; but with all mod cons inside, these were comfy mini-castles, which looked romantic but were practical. No one did them better than Bryce. Examples include Armadale Castle on Skye and Balfour Castle on Orkney.

ALEXANDER 'GREEK' THOMSON (1817–75)

Increasingly regarded as one of the finest architects anywhere, Thomson's body of work is confined to Glasgow and the west of Scotland. His remarkable style blended elements from Greek and Egyptian art to create utterly individual and beautiful buildings, many of which are now lost, and one of which, the Caledonia Road church, exists only as a sad shell in the Gorbals and his lovely Egyptian Halls – a work of world significance – is in trouble (Piloti in *Private Eye* has often commented on its decay). See also Endangered Buildings, p. 204.

SIR ROBERT ROWAND ANDERSON (1834–1921)
Anderson was Scotland's leading architect at the end of the nineteenth century, working in all the styles of the day, from neoclassical to Scottish baronial. He renovated many of Scotland's religious buildings, including Paisley Abbey and Dunfermline Abbey. Mount Stuart on Bute is one of his most striking buildings, an exuberant Gothic palace built for the Marquess of Bute.

CHARLES RENNIE MACKINTOSH (1868–1928)
One of the most influential and popular Scottish architects, Mackintosh was a prominent exponent of art nouveau design and created some of the most outstanding buildings of his day, such as the Glasgow School of Art, the Willow Tearooms (in Sauchiehall Street), Hill House (Helensburgh), and Scotland Street School. The Mackintosh style has been relentlessly copied for what has been dubbed 'Gift Shop Mockintosh'.

—— Endangered Buildings ——

Scotland has a surprisingly large number of endangered buildings of great historical and architectural value, ranging from ancient castles to twentieth-century buildings. The Scottish Civic Trust (funded by Scottish Heritage) maintains an invaluable Buildings at Risk Register for Scotland which lists well over 1,000 buildings of note, including several UNESCO World Heritage Sites: a shameful situation for a small European country in 2008 (the register was established in 1990, since when nearly 1,000 buildings on the list have been rescued through restoration/conversion, with 300 being demolished). Here are just two examples of an endangered Scottish building; there are many more.

St Peter's Seminary
Sited at Cardross near Glasgow, this A-listed seminary was commissioned by the Archbishop of Glasgow in 1958, completed in 1966 and closed in 1980. Described as a modernist masterpiece, and also as Scotland's first major twentieth-century ruin. (NB: if you plan on going to see it, do so in company: it is a lonely place at the end of a lonely path.) In 2007 the World Monument Fund added the building to its list of the world's most endangered buildings. In 2016, the art charity NVA presented a spectacular show called *Hinterland*, 'to reclaim the future' of the Seminary.

The Egyptian Halls, 84–100 Union St, Glasgow
One of Alexander 'Greek' Thomson's remarkable buildings, built 1870–2. It is A-listed yet is in parlous condition.

—— A Few Great Bridges and a Viaduct ——

To end on a cheery note, Scotland has many fine bridges. Here are a few:

Forth Rail Bridge
The most famous cantilever bridge in the world, the 12-mile-long Forth Rail Bridge has been described as 'the one internationally recognised Scottish landmark'. Opened in 1890, it is still running smoothly. The phrase 'painting the Forth Rail Bridge' has long been a colloquial expression

signifying a never-ending task, but in 2008 a new type of paint was developed that will last for at least twenty-five years.

SKYE ROAD BRIDGE
This elegant bridge connecting Kyle of Lochalsh to Skye was opened in 1995 to much controversy, as it was PFI-funded and a toll bridge. After a vigorous campaign by locals, the bridge was bought into public ownership and the tolls were dropped in December 2004. For an analysis of the economics of the PFI funding of the bridge, see George Monbiot's *Captive State* (2001).

TAY RAIL BRIDGE
The first Tay Bridge spanning the Firth of Tay was completed in 1878, and at over 2 miles was one of the longest bridges in the world at the time. The bridge collapsed during a storm in December 1879, taking a train down with it; seventy-five people died, and local poet William Topaz McGonagall wrote one of his famous poems on the subject:

> Beautiful Railway Bridge of the Silv'ry Tay!
> Alas! I am very sorry to say
> That ninety lives have been taken away
> On the last Sabbath day of 1879,
> Which will be remember'd for a very long time.

The replacement bridge was completed in 1887 and remains in use.

GLENFINNAN VIADUCT
Built of concrete at the end of the nineteenth century, the viaduct is known to millions through the Harry Potter films. Both utterly beautiful and functional, the Glenfinnan Viaduct is a fine example of what the Victorians did for us.

And finally ...

THE NOWHERE BRIDGES

Glasgow has ongoing issues with 'Nowhere Bridges'; we will therefore cheat and direct the reader to the Wikipedia entry on the topic: en.wikipedia.org/wiki/M8_Bridge_to_Nowhere

One of the bridges has been completed and is now known as the 'Anderston Footbridge'.

15

Scottish Literature

❖

For such a small nation, Scotland has produced many great writers, but the following list is not a 'Great' list: it seems unlikely, for example, that posterity will rule that Henry Mackenzie (who is in) is a better novelist than Alan Massie or Andrew O'Hagan (who is not), but Mackenzie is part of our literary history in a way that many fine Scots writers are not – quite – yet. Alasdair Gray and Jim Kelman have to be present, as does the Don of 'Tartan Noir', Ian Rankin; indeed, posterity may even decide that crime writers such as Rankin, Christopher Brookmyre and Denise Mina are the real literary stars of the age in Scotland. And why no Alexander McCall Smith? Oh, go on then…

—— Fifty-four Fine Writers ——

ANONYMOUS

'Anonymous' produced some of Scotland's greatest poems, from 'The Twa Corbies' to 'The Ballad of Otterburn'. The Border ballads, in particular, quoted throughout this book, are among the world's greatest lyrics. Sir Philip Sidney said in his *Defense of Poesie* (1595): 'Certainly I must confess mine own barbarousness, I never heard the old song of Percy and Douglas, that I found not my heart moved more than with a trumpet.' Both Burns and Scott drew heavily upon those old traditions and voices. As the great 1907–21 *Cambridge History of English and American Literature* points out, Burns wrote down 'O'er the Moor amang the Heather' from 'the singing of a disreputable female tramp, Jean Glover... which if not largely by Burns, is not all by Jean, and is probably in part founded on an old song'. 'Disreputable' Jean may have been, but it is to the wandering Jean Glovers – whose names we so rarely know – that we owe much of our lyric heritage.

JOHN BARBOUR (c.1330–95)
An Archdeacon of Aberdeen, Barbour is best remembered for his poem *The Bruce* (1375), an epic of over 14,000 lines celebrating the life of Robert the Bruce. The poem is not reliable history but has been very popular with Scots down through the centuries. As the *Dictionary of National Biography* says, 'women are rare in its pages. Its most famous passage is an encomium of freedom, which, it can reasonably be pointed out, in Barbour is enjoyed by men of nobility.'

SIR JAMES MATTHEW BARRIE (1860–1937)
In creating *Peter Pan* (1904), Barrie, like Robert Louis Stevenson, created characters who seem to have always been with us. Barrie gave the copyright to Great Ormond Street Hospital, which continues to benefit from it financially. His other works include a rather creepy supernatural play set on a Hebridean island, *Mary Rose* (1920), and a great novel of class reversal, *The Admirable Crichton* (1902).

BLIND HARRY (c.1440–c.92)
Very little is known about Blind Harry. His epic poem on William Wallace – *The Actes and Deidis of the Illustre and Vallyeant Campioun Schir William Wallace* – was written about 1477 and is one of the main sources for Wallace's life. Burns borrowed the couplet 'A false usurper sinks in every foe/And

liberty returns with every blow' for 'Scots Wha Hae', describing it as a 'couplet worthy of Homer'.

JAMES BOSWELL (1740–95)

His *Life of Samuel Johnson* (1791) is one of the greatest of all biographies, and *A Journal of a Tour to the Hebrides* (1773), his account of travelling to the Hebrides with the crypto-Jacobite Johnson, is enthralling and a valuable record of the Western Isles at that time. Much of Boswell's writing was suppressed by his family after he died because of its sexual explicitness and descriptions, many descriptions, of encounters with prostitutes.

GEORGE DOUGLAS BROWN (1869–1902)

Brown is remembered for one novel, *The House with the Green Shutters* (1901), a grim and realistic portrayal of life in small-town Scotland. The novel is a mortar shell directed at the Kailyard School of writers and has been very influential.

JOHN BUCHAN (1875–1940)

Buchan became 1st Baron Tweedsmuir and Governor-General of Canada (1935–40), but is remembered as the author of such classic adventure novels as *The Thirty-Nine Steps* (1915), *Greenmantle* (1916), and *Sick Heart River* (1941). Buchan's heroes often have an almost mystical relationship with wild country – an empathy drawn from Buchan's own deep feelings for the Scottish hills.

ROBERT BURNS (1759–96)

Burns was born in Ayrshire, worked as a labourer on his father's farm, and later became an excise officer. A convivial drinking companion, Burns soon acquired a reputation as a man 'who loved mankind in general, and women in particular'.

He became famous in 1786 with the publication of the 'Kilmarnock edition' of his poems, *Poems, Chiefly in the Scottish Dialect*. Burns went to Edinburgh to prepare a revised edition, and became the toast of polite society. Scott, then a young boy of sixteen, described him as having a unique 'glowing eye'. Many of Burns's best poems were written while he was still in his twenties: 'The Cotter's Saturday Night', 'The Twa Dogs', 'The Jolly Beggars', 'To a Mouse'. The first of these is written in 'standard' English, the others in Scots, which remained far and away his best medium. Burns wrote some really dull verse in the standard poetic diction of the day – 'Does Haughty Gaul Invasion Threat?' is an especially dire example – but rarely struck a duff note when writing in Scots. A bigger problem for Burnsians is his rather startling willingness, before the success of his poems, to go off to Jamaica to work on the Scottish slave plantations there. Said Burns:

> But before leaving my native land, I resolved to publish my poems. I weighed my productions as impartially as was in my power; I thought they had merit; and it was a delicious idea that I should be called a clever fellow, even though it should never reach my ears – a poor negro-driver – or, perhaps, a victim to that inhospitable clime, and gone to the world of spirits… I was pretty confident my poems would meet with some applause; but, at the worst, the roar of the Atlantic would deafen the voice of censure, and the novelty of West Indian scenes make me forget neglect.

Burns's willingness to work on one of the fearsome Jamaican plantations is not at all easy to explain. Like most men and women of his day he knew the arguments for and against slavery, and even the irascible William Creech, Burns's Edinburgh publisher, campaigned vigorously against slavery. Burns did write (in 1792) an anti-slavery poem, 'The Slave's Lament', and in 1795 wrote the great celebration of equality, 'A Man's a Man for a' That':

> That Man to Man, the world o'er,
> Shall brothers be for a' that.

Burns Suppers – or Burns Nights – are held all over the world on the bard's birthday, 25 January.

THOMAS CARLYLE (1795–1881)

In his day, Carlyle was regarded as an important writer. He wrote like this (from *Sartor Resartus*, 1833–4): 'More legitimate and decisively authentic is Teufelsdrockh's appearance and emergence (we know not well whence) in the solitude of the North Cape… looking over the infinite Brine, like a little blue Belfry (as we figure), now motionless indeed, yet ready, is stirred, to ring quaintest changes…'

This tortured form of writing was dubbed 'Carlylese'.

SAMUEL RUTHERFORD CROCKETT (1860–1914)

Crockett was one of the leading exponents of what was scathingly dubbed the Kailyard School (a 'kailyard' was a cabbage patch beside a country house), a group of Scottish writers who were perceived (sometimes unfairly) as portraying Scotland as a land of couthy folk immersed in gentle sentiment. Crockett's books included *The Stickit Minister* (1893).

ROBERT BONTINE CUNNINGHAME GRAHAM (1852–1936)

Brought up in Perthshire, the son of a Scottish laird and a half-Spanish mother, Cunninghame Graham went to South America at the age of seventeen, where he ranched, took up horse dealing, and explored forests. He became Liberal MP for North-West Lanarkshire in 1886, founding president of the Scottish Labour Party in 1888, and the first socialist MP; he campaigned with Kropotkin, Engels, and George Bernard Shaw, and became first president of the Scottish National Party in 1934.

Cunninghame Graham wrote many fine books, from *Mogreb-el-Acksa* (1898), an account of exploration in Morocco which inspired Shaw's *Captain Brassbound's Conversion*, to *Scottish Stories* (1914) and *The Horses of the Conquest* (1930).

ARTHUR CONAN DOYLE (1859–1930)

Doyle had his first story published in *Chambers Edinburgh Journal* while still a teenager, and continued writing stories while working as a physician. Sherlock Holmes made his first appearance in *A Study in Scarlet*, which appeared in *Beeton's Christmas Annual* (1887). Holmes was an instantly memorable character, and even when Doyle killed him off at the Reichenbach Falls in 1893 ('The Final Problem'), he was forced by public opinion to bring him back. Doyle's other novels include *The White Company* (1891) and *The Lost World* (1912).

CAROL ANN DUFFY (born 1955)

Glasgow-born Duffy was appointed Poet Laureate in 2009, becoming the first Scot, woman, and openly gay person to fill the post. Her poems include the much-loved 'Prayer' ('Darkness outside. Inside, the radio's prayer – Rockall. Malin. Dogger. Finisterre') and 'September 2014', a poignant reflection on the referendum.

WILLIAM DUNBAR (c.1465–c.1513)

Dunbar was a priest who moved in the court circles around

James IV and a major poet. His poems include a fine one on London – 'London, thou art the Flower of cities all' – but his greatest work is 'Lament for the Makaris' (*c.*1507), an elegy mainly for his fellow poets ('makar' is the Scots word for 'poet'), which has the repeated refrain *Timor Mortis conturbat me* ('the fear of death disturbs me').

Four of the poets Dunbar mentions in the poem are in this section: Barbour, Blind Harry, Robert Henryson and Walter Kennedy. In 'The Flyting of Dunbar and Kennedie' (*c.*1508) – flyting is an enjoyable old Scots exercise in which two poets insult each other, rather like rap contests – we have the expression 'Wan-fukkit funling'; and in another poem we find 'Yit be his feirris he wald have fukkit'. These are claimed to be the first appearances of 'fuck' in print.

ROBERT FERGUSSON (*1750–74*)
Fergusson – like Allan Ramsay – has mainly been noted by posterity as an influence on Burns, but he was a hugely talented satirist, his virtuosity in this field being much admired by Burns (who borrowed a whole chunk of Fergusson's verse in 'The Holy Fair'). Fergusson died young, troubled by mental illness, at the age of twenty-four.

SUSAN EDMONSTONE FERRIER (*1782–1854*)
Ferrier wrote three fine novels, *Marriage* (1818), *Inheritance* (1824), and *Destiny* (1831). Scott described her as 'gifted' (Ferrier was a big help to Scott when his memory started to go). Ferrier's reputation has never been as high as it should have been, possibly because she has been described as 'the Scottish Jane Austen', a hard comparison for any author to live up to.

George MacDonald Fraser (1925–2008)

Fraser was born in Carlisle, but like many Borderers had a fluid Anglo-Scottish identity. His best known works are the twelve Flashman novels (1969–2005) which contain many highly perceptive portrayals of a few of the Victorians in this book, such as Sir Colin Campbell. Fraser's other works include the classic study of the Borderers, *The Steel Bonnets* (1971), the great McAuslan stories, collected in *The Complete McAuslan* (2000), and one of the great factual war books, *Quartered Safe Out Here* (1992), his memoir of service with the Border Regiment in Burma.

Lewis Grassic Gibbon (pseudonym of James Leslie Mitchell) (1901–35)

Gibbon's great work is the trilogy *A Scots Quair*, comprising the novels *Sunset Song* (1932), *Cloud Howe* (1933), and *Grey Granite* (1934). The trilogy tells the story of Chris Guthrie, a farm girl, through broken marriages and parenthood to her move to the city. The progress of the work is meant to mirror Marx's theory of history; Chris's son joins the Communist Party and the work ends with a mystical passage in which Chris apparently becomes one with the earth.

Kenneth Grahame (1859–1932)

Grahame wrote some classic children's stories including *The Golden Age* (1895), *Dream Days* (1898), and *The Wind in the Willows* (1908), all composed in his spare time to entertain his son.

Alasdair Gray (born 1934)

Gray is an acclaimed artist as well as one of Scotland's most highly regarded modern authors. His first novel *Lanark* (1981) displays what became his customary mix of naturalistic description, fantasy elements, and his own beautiful illustrations. Gray is a prominent advocate of an independent and socialist Scottish state.

Hamish Henderson (1919–2002)
Henderson is important in several respects: one of the most admired Scots poets of his generation, he was also a huge influence on the folk song revival following the Second World War, during which, despite initial pacifism, he served with the 51st Highland Division. His magnificent anthem 'Freedom Come-All-Ye', which many feel should be Scotland's national anthem, celebrates a future in which all races are equal and there is no oppression 'Through the great glen o' the warld'. Bob Dylan has said the lyric influenced him.

Robert Henryson (died c. 1490)
Henryson studied at Glasgow University and was probably a priest. His best known poems are his *Morall Fabillis of Esope* and *The Testament of Cresseid*. Dunbar's 'Lament for the Makaris' says he died in Dunfermline.

Archie Hind (1928–2008)
Hind's Glasgow novel *The Dear Green Place* (1966) won the *Guardian* prize for First Novel and is now seen as a landmark in Scottish fiction, its hero being a working-class Glaswegian struggling to write about himself and his city.

James Hogg (1770–1835)
Hogg was a self-educated shepherd (dubbed the 'Ettrick Shepherd' by his contemporaries). He became a leading light of the Edinburgh literary scene from 1810 (both Scott and Wordsworth had encouraged him in his writing). Hogg produced some extraordinary works, including a great novel,

The Private Memoirs and Confessions of a Justified Sinner (1824), a dark masterpiece about Calvinist mania and murder, and *The Three Perils of Man* (1822), a wild and wacky precursor of the sword and sorcery genre. He also wrote many good parodies of his fellow poets.

JOHN HOME (1722–1808)

Leith-born Home was a poet, but is chiefly remembered for his play *Douglas* (1756), a blank-verse tragedy that was very popular in both Scotland and England. Its premiere in Edinburgh was eagerly anticipated (though condemned by the Edinburgh clergy), and during the performance a member of the audience exclaimed: 'Whaur's yer Wullie Shakespeare noo?'

ROBIN JENKINS (1912–2005)

Jerkins had a long career as a novelist, from *So Gaily Sings the Lark* (1950), published when he was thirty-eight, to *Lady Magdalen* (2004), published when he was ninety-two. He wrote over thirty novels, many of them highly acclaimed, yet he never achieved the popular success many felt he deserved. His best known novel, *The Cone-Gatherers* (1955), draws on his experiences working for the Forestry Commission during the Second World War (Jenkins was a pacifist and conscientious objector).

JACKIE KAY (born 1961)

Born in Edinburgh to a Scottish mother and Nigerian father, Kay was adopted and her poems often deal with issues of identity. She was appointed Scots Makar (National Poet) in 2016, succeeding Liz Lochhead. She is the former partner of the UK laureate, Carol Ann Duffy.

JAMES KELMAN *(born 1946)*

Kelman's first novel was *The Busconductor Hines* (1984), a novel about a Glaswegian bus conductor written in Glaswegian – notable for being perhaps the first novel to include a recipe for Scottish mince: 'Don't use a frying pan to brown the mince; what you do is...' Kelman won the Booker Prize for *How Late It Was, How Late* (1994). Kelman's style has been endlessly parodied but is actually difficult to replicate; his is a very individual (and very sweary) voice with no obvious forerunners or heirs.

WALTER KENNEDY *(c.1455–c.1518)*

Kennedy seems to have been a landowner (in Carrick) and in minor clerical orders. He is best remembered for his 'flyting' encounter with Dunbar, in which he claims that Gaelic, not English, is 'the gud langage of this land'. However, all his recorded verse is in English.

LIZ LOCHHEAD *(born 1947)*

A poet and playwright whose work has wide appeal, from children to old cynics, Lochhead was appointed Scotland's second Makar in 2011 (succeeded by Jackie Kay in 2016).

VAL MCDERMID *(born 1955)*

Kirkcaldy-born McDermid is one of the most celebrated 'Tartan Noir' crime writers (see also fellow Fifer Ian Rankin). Her peers awarded her the Crime Writers' Association Gold Dagger for Best Crime Novel of the Year in 1995 for *The Mermaids Singing*. She is a Raith Rovers fan and sponsored the 'McDermid Stand' at Stark's Park in honour of her father.

HUGH MACDIARMID (PSEUDONYM OF C. M. GRIEVE) (1892–1978)

He is regarded as the key figure of what he himself dubbed the 'Scottish Renaissance' of the 1920s. MacDiarmid's greatest poem is *The Drunk Man Looks at the Thistle* (1926), a rousing work that influenced many subsequent writers. He was expelled from the Scottish Nationalist Party in the 1920s for being a communist, and soon afterwards was expelled from the Communist Party for nationalist sympathies.

GEORGE MACDONALD (1824–1905)

MacDonald is remembered nowadays for stories for children, notably *At the Back of the North Wind* (1871) and *The Princess and the Goblin* (1872). His fantasy novels *Phantastes* (1858) and *Lilith* (1895) are less well known, but were enormously influential on later fantasy writers, particularly C. S. Lewis and J. R. R. Tolkien.

WILLIAM [TOPAZ] MCGONAGALL (c.1830–c.1920)

Dundee native McGonagall is famous for being a very bad poet, but his verse is so bad it has a kind of awful greatness: the lines do not scan and are dragged down by the stilted poetic diction. His most famous poem is 'The Tay Bridge Disaster' commemorating that bridge's collapse in 1879. His poems were posthumously published as *Poetic Gems* (1934) and *More Poetic Gems* (1963).

HENRY MACKENZIE (1745–1831)

An Edinburgh attorney, Mackenzie is remembered for one unusual novel, *The Man of Feeling* (1771), which he self-published after numerous rejections from publishers. The book was an instant success. The hero is a highly emotional chap, who bursts into tears at every assault on his feelings, as do those people he encounters on his travels. The 1886 edition of the book has a useful index of the different sorts of tears in the book: 'Girl wept, brother sobbed', 'Tears, press-gang could scarce keep from', 'Hand wet by tear just fallen', and so on. *The Man of Feeling* is perhaps not a great novel, but no one else has ever written anything like it.

SORLEY MACLEAN (SOMHAIRLE MACGILL-EAIN) (1911–96)

Born in Raasay, MacLean served with distinction in the Second World War and became one of the leading Gaelic poets of the day, indeed one of the leading poets of his day. His poem 'Hallaig', a meditation on the Highland Clearances, has a great opening line: *'Tha tìm, am fiadh, an coille Hallaig'* ('Time, the deer, is in the wood of Hallaig').

FIONA MACLEOD (PSEUDONYM OF WILLIAM SHARP) (1855–1905)

Sharp wrote Celtic fantasy tales set in the Western Isles (the name 'Fiona' sounds ancient but was actually invented by Sharp). The socialist composer Rutland Boughton made an opera out of his play *The Immortal Hour* (1900), which was the first Glastonbury Festival event in 1916, and became very popular (Betjeman refers to it in 'The Flight from Bootle'). The music is far better than the normal drippy 'celtic' stuff, and Sharp's lyrics – for instance, 'The Faery Song' – are often magnificent. When told that Sharp used to wear a nice frock when he wrote in his 'Fiona MacLeod' persona, the scholar W. P. Ker famously responded: 'Did he? The bitch!'

JAMES MACPHERSON (1736–96)

Macpherson provoked one of the most fraught literary controversies of the eighteenth century by publishing what he said were authentic translations of ancient Scots Gaelic verse: *Fragments of Ancient Poetry* (1760), *Fingal* (1762), and *Temora* (1763), the last two supposedly by an old Highland bard called Ossian.

The poems were massively popular: Goethe quoted them in *The Sorrows of Young Werther*, and Napoleon slept with them under his pillow. As for the authenticity of Ossian, posterity tends to agree with Macpherson's fiercest critic, Dr Johnson: 'The poem of Fingal, he said, was a mere unconnected rhapsody, a tiresome repetition of the same images... "There is neither end or object, design or moral".' (Macpherson and Johnson are buried a few yards apart from each other in Poets' Corner, Westminster Abbey.)

Ossian's popularity has not lasted: W. H. Auden claimed that Ossianic prose is basically advertising language.

EDWIN (GEORGE) MORGAN (1920–2010)
Morgan was one of Scotland's best-loved modern poets, a creator of witty, experimental verse, such as 'The First Men on Mercury', and 'The Loch Ness Monster's Song' (the latter is very popular with children).

EDWIN MUIR (1887–1959)
Muir's poetry includes the much anthologized 'The Child Dying' and 'The Horses'. He was also an acclaimed essayist, and (with his wife Willa) translated Kafka's novels into English.

ALLAN RAMSAY (1684–1758)
Ramsay was brought up on a Lanarkshire farm and dabbled in poetry from an early age. He trained as a wigmaker in Edinburgh and was deeply affected by the 'treachery' of the 1707 Act of Union. He wrote poetry in Scots, and became very successful – his work came out in 'pirate' editions in

London. He asked for a pension in 1722 on the grounds that he was performing a 'national service' by writing in Scots. He remained a passionate anti-Unionist and a barely closeted Jacobite, and was (in his lyric verse) influential on Burns. His son, the portrait painter Allan Ramsay (1713–84), has left a splendid portrait of him.

IAN RANKIN *(born 1960)*

Rankin is the Fife-born author of the Inspector Rebus crime novels set in Edinburgh. The first was *Knots and Crosses* (1987). The Rebus novels (they also feature his protegé, D.S. Siobahn Clarke) are highly regarded as 'police procedurals', and are also fine examples of the dark tradition in Scottish fiction: the American crime novelist James Ellroy called Rankin 'the king of tartan noir'.

JAMES ROBERTSON *(born 1958)*

James Robertson is a writer who deserves special note because of his remarkable novel *Joseph Knight* (2003), the first major work of fiction about Scotland's involvement in slavery. It used to be possible for Scottish academics to write weighty tomes on the Scottish eighteenth-century economy without mentioning Scotland's slave labour force, but after Robertson's novel this is no longer likely. His novel *And the Land Lay Still* (2010) is hailed by many as a remarkably successful depiction of Scotland in the modern era.

J[OANNE] K[ATHLEEN] ROWLING *(born 1965)*

Gloucestershire-born Jo Rowling moved with her infant daughter to Edinburgh in 1993, where she still lives, and where she has written her great series of Harry Potter novels, aided by a grant of £8,000 from the Scottish Arts Council. The Hogwarts School of Witchcraft and Wizardry is located in the Highlands (the Hogwarts Express has made the Glenfinnan Viaduct world famous). Rowling was a prominent 'No' voter during the referendum campaign, for which she was abused by some of the more blood and soil nationalists.

C[HRISTOPHER] J[OHN] SANSOM (born 1952)
A writer of thrillers and the popular historical mystery series of 'Sheldrake' novels, Sansom is also an articulate opponent of Scottish independence. His 'alternate history' novel *Dominion* (2012) depicts a UK ruled by Nazi Germany.

SIR WALTER SCOTT (1771–1832)
Scott's romantic, narrative poems, such as *Marmion* (1808), *The Lady of the Lake* (1810), and *The Lord of the Isles* (1815), attracted immediate critical praise and sold in their thousands. *The Lady of the Lake* (set at Loch Katrine) was particularly successful in Britain and the US, breaking all sales records for poetry, and brought waves of tourists to the loch (the poem is the source for the US presidential anthem, 'Hail to the Chief'). The novels, especially *Waverley* (1814), *The Heart of Midlothian* (1818), and *Ivanhoe* (1819), were also hugely popular. Scott is arguably the most influential writer who ever lived; apart from popularizing Tartan Scotland (by arranging the Edinburgh reception for a kilted George IV in 1822), he had imitators throughout the world who were inspired to create national narratives and costumes for their own lands. Scott was a product of the Scottish Enlightenment and would have been horrified at Mark Twain's suggestion that his works were responsible for the American Civil War (see p. 245).

NAN SHEPHERD (1893–1981)
A novelist and poet, Shepherd also wrote a book on walking in the Cairngorms – *The Living Mountain* – which has become

a much-loved modern classic of nature writing (she wrote it in the forties and chose not to publish it until 1977). In April 2016, her face was chosen to appear on RBS £5 notes.

SYDNEY GOODSIR SMITH (1915–75)
Born in New Zealand, he moved with his family to Edinburgh in 1928. He is regarded as one of the greatest modern Lallans poets, with works such as 'Under the Eildon Tree' (1948). Hugh MacDiarmid wrote the introduction to his *Collected Poems* (1975).

ALEXANDER MCCALL SMITH (born 1948)
Zimbabwe-born Smith is one of the few writers to have created a fictional character who, after a few years, seems to have always been there: the 'traditionally built' heroine of the No. 1 Ladies Detective Agency series, Precious Ramotswe.

MARY SOMERVILLE (1780–1872)
The astronomer Mary Somerville is included in this section as she was a very fine writer who was a mistress of that most complex of tasks: explaining the mysteries of science in clear, well-crafted prose. Oxford's Somerville College is named for her. In February 2016, her face was chosen to appear on RBS £10 notes.

WILLIAM SOUTAR (1898–1943)
Soutar was one of our finest lyric poets (in Scots and standard English) and his poems have often been set to music, most notably by Benjamin Britten in *Who Are These Children?*, a beautiful collection of Soutar settings. Soutar was confined to bed for the rest of his life in 1930 with an incurable spine infection.

Dame Muriel Spark (1918–2006)

Born in Edinburgh to a Jewish father and Anglican mother, Spark converted to Roman Catholicism in 1954, and her religion heavily influenced her novels, which include *The Comforters* (1957), *The Ballad of Peckham Rye* (1960), and *The Prime of Miss Jean Brodie* (1961).

Robert Louis Stevenson (1850–94)

Robert was the grandson of lighthouse designer Robert Stevenson. His first major success was the instant classic *Treasure Island* (1883), followed three years later by *The Strange Case of Dr Jekyll and Mr Hyde* (1886), a fable of dual personality and good and evil that has maintained its grip on our imaginations. His other novels include the immortal Scottish romances, *Kidnapped* (1886), *The Master of Ballantrae* (1889), and the unfinished *Weir of Hermiston* (1896). He also wrote wonderful poems, loved by children as well as adults, and great short stories, such as the Scots masterpiece, 'Thrawn Janet'. Stevenson settled in Samoa, where he died. The Samoans nicknamed him 'Tusitala', 'the Storyteller', and he remains one of the world's favourite storytellers.

Irvine Welsh (born 1956)

Welsh stormed to fame with the publication of *Trainspotting* (1993), a rollercoaster of a novel depicting the lives of young Edinburgh heroin users (one character is addicted to violence rather than heroin). Edinburgh Welsh is often compared to Glasgow Kelman as if they were the same sort of beast, but as Edwin Morgan once pointed out, they are quite, quite different. Kelman gives us a recipe for mince; Welsh gives us a recipe for coming off heroin: 'Ten tins ay Heinz tomato soup…'

16

Legend and the Dark Side

❖

The Scots language has many marvellous words dealing with the supernatural: fey (fairy-like, magical), unco (uncanny, unnatural), unchancy (dangerous), ferlie (marvel), and so on, largely because it needs them, given the bogles and boggarts that lurk in the Scottish mirk. Here are some eldritch (from *elfritch* or *elfrice*, 'fairyland') tales.

—— Fairies ——

FAIRYLAND

Scottish fairies closely resemble Irish and English ones. The Highland fairies, like the Irish ones, are called the Sidhe or Sith: the 'shee', while the Border fairies are pretty much the same as the Northumberland ones (typical Borderers; they probably have cross-border clans like the Grahams and Armstrongs). They are all little people, they all live under the hills, they were here before us, and they mostly don't care for us very much. Occasionally they swap a sickly unwanted child of theirs with one of ours – a **changeling**. Some of them may be a bit easier to get on with than others: **Brownies** will often do household chores in return for left-out snacks, but even at their friendliest they are unchancy folk, best kept at a distance.

Rationalists say the Scottish fairies are possibly our folk memory of the Picts, who were traditionally regarded as 'dwarfish';

in other words, little people who had hidden, secret knowledge (such as how to make heather ale). In this view, Scots feel guilt for wiping out the Picts, and the fairies are our self-punishment: small dark creatures lurking within the bogs of the Scottish collective unconscious. It is true that Scottish fairies may seem even more ill-natured than English ones, but fairies, from whatever ancestral shadows they may come, don't really need reasons to dislike us – they just do.

In both Scottish and English supernatural traditions, descriptions of fairies can mean the opposite of what they say: Scots used to call the devil the 'Guidman', and just as the Ancient Greeks referred to the Fates as the Eumenides – the 'Kindly Ones' – when they were of course not friendly at all, so fairyland is referred to as 'fair', when it is really anything but fair and lovely. Susanna Clarke's fine novel *Jonathan Strange and Mr Norrell* (2004), is the best modern guide to the strange, chilly and joyless realm of fairyland that our forebears believed existed on the 'other side'.

THE FAIRY FLAG
In Dunvegan Castle there hangs a very old tattered piece of silk: the Fairy Flag. The flag has been in the MacLeod of MacLeod family for centuries, and legend says it came into the clan through a fairy wife who used it to wrap her baby in. It has been waved in times of crisis or battle by the MacLeod clan. The MacLeod clan is Viking in origin, and it has been suggested that the flag may be a Viking 'Landwaster' Raven Banner – Earl Sigurd of Orkney was killed at Clontarf in 1014, carrying such a banner. The flag has been dated to between the fourth and seventh centuries and has a Middle Eastern origin. However, a supernatural origin can still be argued for: Vikings fought and traded in the Middle East and often made

strategic marriages, so perhaps a MacLeod ancestor married a Syrian with a djinn in the family.

TAM LIN

Tam Lin is a Border ballad about a fairy knight, Tam Lin, who guards a wood called Carterhaugh, where he demands the virginity of maids who pass through. A laird's daughter falls in love with him; Tam explains that he was once an earthly knight and he can be freed if she manages to hold on to him while he changes shape. She holds him as he turns into all manner of awful things, throws him into a well when he explodes into flames, then covers him with her green mantle – and wins her knight. The Queen of the Fairies (keeking from a bush) is not pleased and doesn't give Tam up gracefully:

> Shame betide her ill-far'd face,
> And an ill death may she die,
> For she's taen awa the bonniest knight
> In a' my companie.
>
> 'But had I kenned, Tam Lin,' said she,
> 'What now this night I see,
> I wad hae taen out thy twa grey een,
> And put in twa een o tree.'

THE REVEREND ROBERT KIRK

Robert Kirk (or Kirke) was minister of Aberfoyle in the 1680s, whom Sir Walter Scott later described as 'a man of some talents, who translated the Psalms into Gaelic verse' (Kirk's parishioners were Gaelic-speaking). Kirk is best known, however, for his book *The Secret Commonwealth of Elves, Fauns and Fairies. Or, a Treatise displayeing the Chiefe Curiosities as they are in Use among diverse of the People of Scotland to this Day; Singularities for the most Part peculiar to that Nation* (written 1691, published 1815).

Kirk was a seventh son, and his tomb can be seen in the Old Kirk, Aberfoyle. Above the town is Doon Hill, where he was found dead. Another tradition says that the tomb is in fact empty; Doon Hill is a fairy hill, and the fairies took him for giving away their secrets. Says Scott:

> Shortly after his funeral, he appeared, in the dress in which he had sunk down, to a medical relation of his own, and of Duchray. 'Go,' said he to him, 'to my cousin Duchray, and tell him that I am not dead. I fell down in a swoon, and was carried into Fairyland, where I now am. Tell him, that when he and my friends are assembled at the baptism of my child (for he had left his wife pregnant), I will appear in the room, and that if he throws the knife which he holds in his hand over my head, I will be released and restored to human society.' The man, it seems, neglected, for some time, to deliver the message. Mr. Kirke appeared to him a second time, threatening to haunt him night and day till he executed his commission, which at length he did. The time of the baptism arrived. They were seated at table; the figure of Mr. Kirke entered, but the Laird of Duchray, by some unaccountable fatality, neglected to perform the prescribed ceremony. Mr. Kirke retired by another door, and was seen no more. It is firmly believed that he is, at this day, in Fairyland.

—— Two Wizards ——

MICHAEL SCOT OR SCOTT (died c.1235)

The historical Michael Scot was a theologian who studied at Oxford and Toledo, and was possibly court astrologer to Emperor Frederick II. He died in Italy and legends rapidly spread about him: Dante describes him in the eighth circle of hell in the *Inferno* – 'Michael Scot, for magic arts renowned' – and he also appears in Boccaccio's *Decameron*. In Scottish (and Italian) legend, Scot became one of the greatest wizards of them all. In Walter Scott's *The Lay of the Last Minstrel* (Scott claimed Scot as a relation) he describes him as having 'cleft the Eildon hills in three and bridled the river Tweed with a curb of stone' – thus creating the three peaks that overlook Melrose.

SIR WILLIAM DE SOULIS *(died c.1320)*

As it may well be the grimmest castle in the world (see p. 196), the keep of Hermitage should have dark legends attached to it, and indeed it does. The castle was owned for many years by the Norman de Soulis family, one of whom, Sir William de Soulis, was reputed to be a wizard. His reign of terror over Liddesdale and the Debatable Land was brought to an end by locals who wrapped him in sheets of lead and boiled 'the Bad Lord Soulis' to death in the stone circle on Ninestane Rigg:

> On a circle of stone they placed the pot,
> On a circle of stones but barely nine,
> They heated it up red and fiery hot,
> Till the burnished brass did glimmer and shine.
>
> They rolled him up in a sheet of lead,
> A sheet of lead for a funeral pall,
> They plunged him in the cauldron red,
> And melted him, lead, bones and all.

Another tradition says Thomas the Rhymer disposed of him in the same manner. Soulis was aided in his depredations by a fearful spirit called Robin Redcap. Robin is still about, it is said, and every seven years Soulis rises from beneath the stone circle for a tryst with him. The legend is linked to the historical

Sir William de Soulis, who was 'Butler of Scotland' and whose seal is affixed to the Declaration of Arbroath (see Appendix A). De Soulis died while imprisoned in Dumbarton Castle, *c.*1320.

—— Second Sight ——

The second sight is an extrasensory vision of an event that will happen in the future. It is said to be a special gift of seventh sons of seventh sons. Here are two Scots who were said to have the gift of prophecy:

Thomas the Rhymer

Thomas the Rhymer was a real person called Thomas of Ercildoune (a village just north of Melrose), who lived during the late thirteenth century. Two signatures on charters survive of this historical 'Thome Rimor de Ercildun'. Thomas acquired a reputation as a prophet from the fifteenth century onwards. He made lots of prophecies, including the Scots defeat at Flodden in 1513, and the Act of Union in 1707, but as no one thought to write any of these down before they happened, most Scottish historians are sceptical. Thomas was taken by the Queen of Fairyland for seven years:

> O they rade on, and farther on,
> And they waded rivers abune the knee;
> And they saw neither sun nor moon,
> But they heard the roaring of the sea.

The Brahan Seer

The Brahan Seer, also known as Coinneach Odhar or Kenneth Mackenzie, is said to have lived in the seventeenth century and to have been employed (for his wit and gifts of prophecy) at Brahan Castle (near Dingwall) by the Mackenzie chief, the

3rd Earl of Seaforth. The earl died in 1678, and legend says the seer was burned in a tar barrel by Lady Seaforth for saying the earl was unfaithful – so if the seer existed, he must have died in or before 1678. He made many wonderfully specific and often highly mundane prophecies: for example, that a certain church roof would collapse if a magpie built its nest on it three years running; that a rock would fall over; and – many people's favourite – that a Frenchman would die on a Scots island and be mourned by a woman. He foretold that the last heir of the ruling Mackenzie line would be deaf, which came to pass. Sadly, as with Thomas the Rhymer, none of this was written down before it happened. His prophecies are collected in *The Prophecies of the Brahan Seer* (1899) by Alexander Mackenzie. More modern 'Brahan Seer' prophecies, such as North Sea oil rigs, are not in the canon.

—— Water Spirits ——

A **water horse** or *each uisge*, ('ech ooshka') is a shape-shifting spirit that lives in lochs. Water horses are dangerous, and often take the form of a fine-looking horse, or a handsome man, to tempt the unwary closer. Once captured, the victim is taken to the bottom of the loch to be devoured. Water horses may or may not have anything to do with the well-known monsters who inhabit Scottish lochs such as Lochs Ness, Morar, and Shiel.

One of the few records we have of a loch monster attacking anyone is in Adamnan's biography of Columba. In this case, Nessie seems to have been attacking people in the river, and rivers and streams are where **kelpies** generally live. Kelpies are said to be not as dangerous as water horses but few, if any, water spirits in European culture are benign. Give them all a wide berth.

SELKIES

Selkies are beings that can shape-shift from seal to human form and back again. They often form relationships with humans, but selkie–human love stories rarely end well. Avoid any potential partners who have a strong attachment to seal-skin clothing, as selkies keep their old skins with them and are liable to slip back into them at unexpected moments.

—— Horrible Earthly Spirits ——

HUGBOYS AND TROWS

… and **Wulvers**, **Redcaps**, **Dunters** and **Powries**. Apart from fairies under the hill and water horses and kelpies in the water, there are some really awful things lurking in the Scottish countryside. Hugboys are scary spirits native to Orkney which live in old burial mounds and they sometimes share their neighbourhoods with trows, or trolls, which live in mounds called Trowie Knowes. Trows are nasty, brutish, and short, and are also found on Shetland. A trow called Nikademius lives on 'Da Sneck o da Smallie' on the Shetland isle of Foula: don't visit him at night. The wulver is a Shetland werewolf variant. They don't seem to shift form: the permanent form is a man's body and a wolf's head. Wulvers spend a lot of time fishing and have occasionally been described as benevolent, leaving fish for poor families.

Redcaps are Border beings, also called dunters and powries, which may be localized variants of redcaps. They have sharp claws and get their name because they want to dip their hats in your blood. They will outrun you. If you meet one your only hope is to chant bits of the Bible at it, and its teeth will fall out. Dunters are particularly associated with castles, and may be guardian spirits (read M. R. James), or possibly the grounded souls of humans sacrificed at the building's foundation. The wizard Sir William de Soulis was accompanied by a redcap called Robin.

—— The Ninth Legion ——

The Roman Army's Ninth Legion was raised by Julius Caesar for the Gallic Wars around 60 BC, and vanished in the second century AD. The legion's Roman name is Legio VIIII Hispana, and it probably earned its name from fighting in Spain, rather than being raised there. Scottish legend has it that the legion was annihilated fighting against the Caledonian tribes, but this is debatable. The legion was last recorded in York around AD 70 and then transferred to Germania where it may have been wiped out in a second-century revolt. Rosemary Sutcliffe's classic children's novel *An Eagle of the Ninth* (1954) sticks to the myth and has sold over a million copies (it is actually a fine read and an excellent introduction to that wild frontier world).

—— The Beast of Glamis ——

Glamis is a beautiful, ancient castle with a dark legend attached. The 'beast' or 'monster' is supposed to have been a member of the Bowes-Lyon family, Thomas Bowes-Lyon, who is recorded as having been born in 1821 and dying soon after. The legend relates that Thomas did not die, but was so horribly deformed that he was kept secluded in one of the castle's secret rooms until his death. The details of the story can be found in *The Queen Mother's Family Story* (1967), by James Wentworth-Day. The 'monster' features in many works of fiction, most recently in the comic-book series 'The Invisibles' as a 200-year-old Moonchild.

—— The Stone of Destiny ——

The story of the Stone of Destiny (also known as the 'stone of Scone', pronounced 'skoon') seems straightforward enough. According to the most popular legend, it was the biblical Jacob's 'pillow stone' and had been used by the ancestors of the Scots to crown their kings upon. It is possible that Kenneth MacAlpin was crowned upon it, as were all succeeding Scottish kings until Edward I stole it from Scone Abbey in 1296 and took it to Westminster Abbey. The stone was pinched by three Scottish students in 1950 and went back to Westminster in 1951. In 1996 the stone was finally returned for good to Scotland and now lives in Edinburgh Castle. But is it the real stone? A popular tradition has it that the stone taken by Edward was a planted fake – an old door lintel, or even cesspit cover, carved out of the local red sandstone. It is perfectly plausible that the real stone is still hidden somewhere around Scone.

17

The Clan System and Tartan

❖

—— Clans ——

The late Dame Flora MacLeod of MacLeod (1878–1976) was fond of telling MacLeods from abroad that their ancestors may well have climbed 'these very steps' themselves, as they ascended the splendid staircase in Dunvegan Castle. Perhaps, but it was unlikely.

The word 'clan' derives from the Gaelic 'clann', 'children', and, in theory at least, chieftainship was held with the consent of the 'children'. In fact, whatever the original system may have been (the earliest recorded clans seem to have all disappeared by the sixteenth century), as we enter historical times, Highland clans were heavily influenced by the feudal systems of rule established by Vikings, and also, from the eleventh century, the Normans. These medieval Scottish clans, whether in the Hebrides like the MacLeods, or inland like the Frasers, were made up of a territorial network of people who may have been (but not always) related to each other, and with a hierarchy of leadership topped by a boss man.

Observers of old Highland life agree that resources were scarce, and present-day Somalia is a comparable society to the sixteenth-century Highlands, where people of the same religion and same belief systems coexist in groups engaging in 'resource wars' with each other. Bands of Highland warriors would extend the snatching of resources by raiding the Lowlands in a cattle-raiding spreidh (which is where we get the word 'spree', as in 'shopping spree'), but these consumer trips could end in death.

The romantic image of the '45 is of Cameron of Lochiel welcoming Bonnie Prince Charlie at Glenfinnan amid skirling pipes and loyal warriors, but the reality was Lochiel's brutal brother Archibald forcing the Cameron 'children' to join the rebellion by threatening to burn their houses. Charlie's Cameron contingent was obtained by the simple expedient of whipping men and killing livestock.

In Walter Scott's *Waverley*, a father willingly sends his sons to die for the chief, Fergus MacIvor, but Scott's narrator also sees the murky confusion of the clan system within the Jacobite forces:

> Thus the M'Couls, though tracing their descent from Comhal, the father of Finn, or Fingal, were a sort of... hereditary servants to the Stuarts of Appine. The Macbeaths, descended from the unhappy monarch of that name, were subjects to the Morays, and clan Donnachy, or Robertsons of Athole; and many other examples might be given, but for hurting any pride of clanship which may be left, and thereby drawing a Highland tempest into the shop of my publisher.

Scott's MacIvor was based on Alexander Ranaldson Macdonell of Glengarry, a monster of selfishness who exploited his 'children' in a pitiless manner. In truth, clan leaders such as Glengarry and the Camerons had always behaved like this with the expendable 'children', but after Culloden the chiefs had to answer to courts of Scottish law, as Glengarry had to do. The day of the clan chiefs was over and good riddance.

—— Tartan ——

In Charles Frazier's novel *Thirteen Moons* (2006) a Highland Scot in North Carolina laments the victory of the cruel 'Angles and Saxons' at Culloden over the Scots, the Scots being clad in their 'particular plaiding'. In the real world, the North Carolina Highlanders were overwhelmingly Loyalist (in Virginia, Loyalists were called the 'Scotch Party') – and what Americans often call 'plaid', the Scots call tartan, a plaid in Scotland being a blanket or cloak.

It is often said or implied that Sir Walter Scott invented modern tartan dress in his role as creator of the pageant to welcome King George IV to Edinburgh in 1822. Not quite: the Highland Society of London began asking clan chiefs for their authentic tartans in 1815, a request that produced this perplexed response from Baron MacDonald: 'Being really ignorant of what is exactly The Macdonald Tartan, I request you will have the goodness to exert every Means in your power to Obtain a perfectly genuine Pattern.'

A market had come into being, and myth-makers and entrepreneurs rushed to fill it with fables and goods. The most notable exploiters of the new and profitable tartan market were two glorious impostors called John and Charles Allen who claimed to have Stuart ancestry, and who published a guide to tartan in 1842 called *Vestiarium Scoticum*. The book has been described by one modern historian as full of 'fantasy and bare-faced forgery', yet it remains the ultimate source for many tartan traditions.

The world's first colour photograph, in 1861, was of a tartan ribbon, and by then the tartan industry was in full garish bloom. The oldest tartan design is actually shared with England, the Northumbria or Border tartan – a tasteful black and white check.

THE SCOTS ABROAD

❖

—— Highland Soldiers and ——
the British Empire

The role of Highland troops in establishing and holding the British Empire has long been recognized, but they were not terribly well appreciated at first. In a famous 1753 letter written in Banff (Canada) and addressed to a fellow officer in Nova Scotia, James Wolfe described the Highland troops in the British Army thus: 'I should imagine that two or three independent Highland Companies might be of use; they are hardy, intrepid, used to a rough country and no great mischief if they fall. How can you better employ a secret enemy than by making his end conducive to the common good?'

The letter has been much quoted (with great indignation) and used as an example of how the Highlanders were exploited and used to build the Evil Empire. What is forgotten is that Wolfe had served eight years before at Culloden, and believed, as did other Hanoverian officers (Scots and English), the untrue rumour that the Jacobite troops had been ordered to give no quarter. Wolfe's distaste was shared by the French. The French regarded the Highland troops in Canada as 'Sauvages d'Ecosse', men who neither gave nor wanted quarter – and to compound the insult, they also praised the British soldiers as brave 'English Lions' prior to discovering they were the dreaded Highlanders. Five years later, in 1758, however, Wolfe's views had undergone a transformation. He wrote to Lord Halifax (while, pleasingly, arriving at Halifax, Nova Scotia): 'Fraser's and Brigadier Lawrence's Battalions are here, and both in goodly condition. The Highlanders are very useful serviceable soldiers, and commanded by the most manly corps of officers I ever saw.'

This approving view was not shared in 1762 by elements of the London mob whom Boswell saw in Covent Garden Opera House hissing at two Highland officers, and yelling 'No Scots! No Scots!' Boswell leapt to their defence, shouting, '"Damn you, you rascals!"… I hated the English.' (To be fair to the mob, the despised Scotsman Lord Bute was Prime Minister.)

As Neil Davidson shows in his *The Origins of Scottish Nationhood* (2000), several forces were at work by the 1760s: Highland and Lowland Scots, as Boswell's reaction shows, were beginning to see themselves as a people with a shared identity, the English lower orders didn't like being ruled by dreich Scottish prime ministers, and Highland troops had become a decisive part of the British army. In 1773 a British pamphleteer summed up the Highland contribution thus: 'The reduction of Louisburgh, Quebec, Crown Point, Montreal, Niagara, and Fort de Quesne, the taking of Guadaloupe, the conquest of Martinico, and the Havana, the plains of Germany and our conquest in India, will all tell what assistance the government received from the Scots Highlanders.'

Carving out the empire was not just a matter of fighting, however.

AN ENGINEER, SOLDIER AND SCHOLAR:
COLIN MACKENZIE (1753–1821)
Mackenzie was born in Lewis, and served in India as an engineer and surveyor. He was a popular and brave officer;

Sir Arthur Wellesley (the future Duke of Wellington) said he 'never saw a more zealous, a more diligent, or a more useful officer'. Mackenzie's 'bravery and *sangfroid* in action were proverbial' and his engineering skills played a major part in the defeat of Tipu Sultan in the war of 1798–9. He later became the first Surveyor-General of India. Mackenzie had a wide circle of friends, including Indians, and a deep interest in Indian history, becoming a collector of ancient manuscripts which he had translated with the aid of Brahmins and other learned men. He studied and made drawings of the great Stupa at Amaravati, and played an important part in the rediscovery of India's Buddhist history.

AN AUSTRALIAN GOVERNOR: LACHLAN MACQUARIE (1762–1824)

Macquarie was born in the small island of Ulva, by Mull, and became Governor of New South Wales, 1810–21. Macquarie's rule as governor has been described as that of an 'enlightened despot', but his decisive role in transforming New South Wales from a penal dumping ground to a free colony is undoubted. He returned to Scotland and is buried in the Macquarie mausoleum on Mull, where his grave bears the inscription 'Father of Australia'.

AN EXPLORER: MUNGO PARK (1771–1806)

Mungo Park was born in Selkirk, into a poor tenant family and had a Calvinist upbringing. A classic 'lad o pairts', he attended Selkirk Grammar School, then Edinburgh University, where he studied medicine and botany. In 1795 Park was sent into Africa by the African Association, which was dedicated to 'opening' up Africa to British science and commerce, and its members were also firmly opposed to both Western and Arab slavery (modern apologists for the empire stress the science and the anti-slavery aspect, while anti-imperialists stress the commerce angle and the imperial 'Scramble for Africa' which came in the nineteenth century).

Park discovered the course of the Niger and his book *Travels in the Interior of Africa* (1799) sold well. The British government asked him to lead an expedition back to find the source of the Niger, and Park drowned in the river after the last of many attacks from locals; none of his party survived, apart from one slave who told the tale.

A MISSIONARY: DAVID LIVINGSTONE (1813–73)

Born in Blantyre, Livingstone became one of Britain's most popular heroes, bringing Christianity to Africa, being the first European to see the Victoria Falls, and campaigning vigorously against Arab slavers.

A Congregationalist, Livingstone had originally hoped to go to China, but the London Missionary Society sent him to Africa instead. He was attacked and almost killed by a lion in 1844, and was saved by an African colleague (he recorded that he felt no pain and deduced that this was proof of God's kindness to prey animals).

Livingstone was a distinguished explorer, but regarded his anti-slavery work as much more important. In a letter to the *New York Herald*, he wrote: 'if my disclosures … should lead to the suppression of the East Coast slave trade, I shall regard that as a greater matter by far than the discovery of all the Nile sources together.' Unfortunately, Livingstone depended on the very Arab slave traders he was campaigning against, and at one point was being sent slaves to use as porters.

The journalist Henry Morton Stanley was sent to 'discover' Livingstone by the *New York Herald*, but the famous greeting,

'Dr Livingstone, I presume,' is entirely apocryphal.

Livingstone has been a controversial figure: he was a major player in laying Africa open to exploitation and conquest, and he made few converts to Christianity. But his statues in Zimbabwe and Zambia stand, and in Africa, at least, he is seen as a positive figure.

AN AUSTRALIAN EXPLORER: JOHN MCDOUALL STUART (1815–66)

Born in Fife, in 1862 he became the first known human to cross the centre of Australia from south to north and back. As the editor of The Journals of John McDouall Stuart (1864) put it, the journey is 'amongst the most important in the history of Australian discovery'.

AN INDIAN FIGHTER: RANALD MACKENZIE (1840–89)

Ranald Mackenzie was born (of Scottish descent) in New York and served with distinction in the Civil War. General Grant called him 'the most promising young officer in the army'; his troops, however, called him the 'perpetual punisher', a description the Indians he fought against would have echoed. Mackenzie had lost two fingers on one hand in the war, and the Plains Indians nicknamed him 'Three Fingers' Mackenzie. He became the most successful of all American Indian fighters: campaigning against the Comanche and other Plains Indians, he destroyed villages, he slaughtered the pony herds, he killed all who resisted – and also saved a lot of lives. Mackenzie's 'pacification' campaigns have been compared to those of government troops in the eighteenth-century Highlands, but in truth they seem much the same as Sherman's brutal Civil War campaign against the Southern whites in Georgia.

CONSERVATIONIST: JOHN MUIR (1838–1914)

Not all Scots wandering about the American west in the nineteenth century were busy killing Indians; John Muir, born in Dunbar, became one of the world's leading conservationists. He was also an inventor, who designed and built a water-powered mill, and was a knowledgeable amateur scientist. Muir saved the Yosemite Valley from exploitation and in 1892 founded the Sierra Club, one of America's most influential conservation groups.

—— The Scotch-Irish ——

Many Scots are baffled when Americans talk about the 'Scotch-Irish'. What Americans mean by 'Scotch-Irish' are the eighteenth-century immigrants from Ulster, who were themselves descended from seventeenth-century Scottish emigrants to Ulster, the 'Scottish Plantation' of troublesome Border families such as Nixons, Johnstons, and Armstrongs. (After the moon landing in 1969, President Nixon, Vice-President Johnson – whose family had misplaced the 't' – and Neil Armstrong brought these Border names together on American television.)

The Scotch-Irish came over in their tens of thousands; they regarded the Catholic Irish, the Anglican English, and the Native Americans with equal malice. They treasured their blood feuds with each other, and also their ancestral memories of city sieges and last stands in hill forts surrounded by cruel enemies: when the Bowies and the Crocketts flocked to the Alamo in 1836, they were entering ancestral psychic territory. In 1776 the Scotch-Irish turned out in their thousands for the Rebels, and without these hard men – men such as the Overmountain Boys who won the Battle of Kings Mountain – the

American Revolution would have failed (Hillary Clinton, Barack Obama, and John McCain all share Scots-Irish descent). The Highlanders mostly sided with the British, while the other Scots were, like their neighbours, tragically divided.

—— Sir Walter Scott and the —— American Civil War

In *Life on the Mississippi* (1883), Mark Twain accused Sir Walter Scott of causing the American Civil War. Twain knew Scott was a good man, and he knew there were other more immediate factors, but he was nonetheless perfectly serious (see also p. 157):

> Then comes Sir Walter Scott with his enchantments, and by his single might checks this wave of progress, and even turns it back; sets the world in love with dreams and phantoms; with decayed and swinish forms of religion; with decayed and degraded systems of government; with the sillinesses and emptinesses, sham grandeurs, sham gauds, and sham chivalries of a brainless and worthless long-vanished society. He did measureless harm; more real and lasting harm, perhaps, than any other individual that ever wrote.

—— Emigration and the Clearances ——

Boswell records that one evening while he and Johnson were guests at Armadale on Skye:

> We performed, with much activity, a dance which, I suppose, the emigration from Sky has occasioned. They call it 'America'. Each of the couples, after the common involutions and evolutions, successively whirls round

in a circle, till all are in motion; and the dance seems intended to shew how emigration catches, till a whole neighbourhood is set afloat. Mrs M'Kinnon told me, that last year when a ship sailed from Portree for America, the people on shore were almost distracted when they saw their relations go off; they lay down on the ground, tumbled, and tore the grass with their teeth. This year there was not a tear shed. The people on shore seemed to think that they would soon follow. This indifference is a mortal sign for the country.

Emigration had become a part of Highland life by the time Boswell and Johnson visited the Western Isles in 1773. Johnson noted this innkeeper's indignant comment: 'From him we first heard of the general dissatisfaction, which is now driving the Highlanders into the other hemisphere; and when I asked him whether they would stay at home, if they were well treated, he answered with indignation, that no man willingly left his native country.'

The eighteenth century was an age of 'improvement' and this was how landlords and clan chiefs saw the situation: glens full of hungry unprofitable people could be replaced with fat profitable sheep.

In England, there had earlier been the 'enclosures', the seizure by landowners of what had once been common land, and similar forces had been at work in the Scottish Lowlands. The difference with the Highland Clearances is that the very existence of Highland culture became endangered by the clearing of the hills and glens for sheep. And the eviction process was often accompanied by much brutality: in Sutherland, 1814 is still remembered as 'the Year of the Burnings'.

As can be seen in this section, and throughout this book, the emigrating Highlanders shaped the modern world, and the old clan-based Highland society was no longer tenable. But without the Clearances, and with the humane aspects of the Scottish Enlightenment and the crypto-Jacobite sympathies of English Toryism at work, a healthy, modern Highland culture could have evolved: and the glens need not have become empty and silent.

For the Clearances, see James Hunter, *Set Adrift from the World: The Sutherland Clearances* (2015). For the chequered history of land ownership in Scotland see Andy Wightman's *The Poor Had No Lawyers: Who Owns Scotland and How They Got It* (2015).

Appendix A

THE DECLARATION OF ARBROATH

❖

'This is the West, sir. When the legend becomes fact, print the legend.'
The Man Who Shot Liberty Valance

The 'Declaration of Arbroath' is the name now commonly given to a letter addressed to the Pope proclaiming Scotland's independence from England. It was drawn up – possibly by the Abbot of Arbroath – on 6 April 1320, and sent to Pope John XXII. The letter (just the one copy survives) was written in Latin and bears the seals of eight earls and forty-one other nobles. The most commonly quoted translation was done by Sir James Fergusson (and the copyright belongs to the National Archives of Scotland, who kindly gave permission for extracts to be used).

The background to the letter is complex. Bruce had been excommunicated by the Pope for the murder of John Comyn (see p. 53), and tensions between England and Scotland were constant; Edward's overlordship of Scotland had been recognized by the Pope in 1305 (indeed, Bruce himself recognized it when it suited him). Scotland was placed under Interdict by the Pope in 1317.

The letter prompted the Pope (who was also receiving complaints about the Scots from the English) to ask Edward to make peace, but the excommunication of Bruce was renewed in 1323 (finally lifted in 1328, as was the Interdict on Scotland).

The Declaration of Arbroath became, in the late 20th century, regarded as one of the iconic landmarks in Scottish history. It is also frequently said that the Declaration was a prototype of contractual kingship in Europe. In fact, the Coronation Oath of Edward II, 25 February 1308 – twelve years prior to the Arbroath Declaration – concludes with this solemn promise:

> 'Sire, do you grant to be held and observed the just laws and customs that the community of your realm shall determine, and will you, so far as in you lies, defend and strengthen them to the honour of God?'

The words 'that the community of your realm shall determine' are clearly contractual in their nature, are perfectly clear about laws being created by the people for the king to follow, and carry a perfectly visible warning – Edward will have to watch his step.

The most famous words in the Declaration of Arbroath are '… as long as but a hundred of us remain alive, never will we on any conditions be brought under English rule. It is in truth not for glory, nor riches, nor honours that we are fighting, but for freedom – for that alone, which no honest man gives up but with life itself.'

Stirring words, but the letter also celebrates genocide and ethnic cleansing: 'The Britons they first drove out, the Picts they utterly destroyed', and – even by medieval standards – is extraordinarily boastful. The Scots have such 'high qualities' that Christ took special notice of them, sending St Andrew to protect them 'forever'.

In 1998, the US Senate agreed that the Scots were special, and designated 6 April to be celebrated each year as 'National Tartan Day' in commemoration of the signing of the

Declaration of Arbroath, and in 2005, Congress passed House Resolution 41:

> 'Whereas April 6 has a special significance for all Americans, and especially those Americans of Scottish descent, because the Declaration of Arbroath, the Scottish Declaration of Independence, was signed on April 6, 1320, and the American Declaration of Independence was modeled in part on that inspirational document...'

Legend (and recent legend at that) has here become fact. It was the egregious right-wing Senator Trent Lott who persuaded Congress and Senate of this influence, an influence confidently repeated on many websites, in books, and in newspaper articles. This influence seems unlikely. There has been, for example, an agreeable suggestion that Jefferson had a Scots nanny who 'must' have told him about the document and he remembered this when drafting the Declaration of Independence, but this is most improbable. In fact, Jefferson may not have been that fond of Scots; he had to be persuaded (by the Scot Witherspoon) to take out a derogatory reference to Scots in his first draft of the DOI, in which he accused the British of sending over 'Scotch & foreign mercenaries to invade & deluge us in blood'. The dominant influence on Jefferson, has long been recognized to be the philosopher John Locke; Thomas Reid (see The Scottish Enlightenment, p. 113) may well have been one of many other influences.

One of the medieval nobles whose seal is affixed to the letter – 'William Soules' – was Sir William de Soulis, who in old legend became one of Scotland's most notorious wizards – a fate that would possibly have pleased him more than becoming the joint-inspirer of a modern legend that he may not have understood: and, ruthless lord that he undoubtedly was, would have despised if he did. Sir William and his temporary allies belong to the world of *The Sopranos*, not the *West Wing*.

In 2016, the Declaration was placed on UNESCO's 'Memory of the World' register.

Appendix B

THE INEVITABLE LIST OF SCOTTISH INVENTIONS, DISCOVERIES, AND INNOVATIONS

❖

It is not true that Russians share a love of Irn-Bru (see p. 152) with the Scots but both countries do seem to share a liking for lists of inventions; in Scotland these are often printed on tea towels for some reason. There are exhaustive – completely exhaustive – lists of Scottish inventions on the web, as can be discovered by googling 'Scottish inventions' (though not all such lists are fully accurate).

Just as the very English J. K. Rowling is now classed by many as a Scottish writer because she lives in Scotland (and got a Scottish Arts Council grant), so Scottish inventiveness is a somewhat broad concept: Glaswegian Robert Foulis invented the foghorn and installed it in Canada; Joseph Lister was English and pioneered antiseptics in Glasgow. Both innovations are generally (and fairly) classed as Scottish, so here they are, along with eighteen other inventive and flexibly Scottish highlights.

1614: LOGARITHMS
John Napier of Merchiston introduced logarithms to a grateful world in his work *Mirifici Logarithmorum Canonis Descriptio* (1614). A gifted mathematician, Napier also had a reputation as a sorcerer.

1694: BANK OF ENGLAND

The bank was founded by Tinwald-born William Paterson (1658–1719). Paterson was also a proponent of the disastrous 1690s Darien Scheme, the failed Scottish colony in Panama which weakened the Scottish economy and is regarded as one of the causes of the 1707 Act of Union.

1718: BANK OF FRANCE

The Banque Générale of France was founded by the Fife-born economist John Law (1671–1729). This bank became the Banque Royale in 1718, its notes being guaranteed by Louis XV.

1747: CURE FOR SCURVY

The Royal Navy Edinburgh-born surgeon James Lind (1716–94) was not the first person to suggest that citrus fruits could be the cure for the dreaded disease of scurvy, but in 1747 he proved his point through a series of experiments – regarded as among the first clinical experiments in medical history. His *A Treatise of the Scurvy* (1753) was ignored at first but gradually became influential. Lind also proved that fresh water could be distilled from sea water.

1768–71: ENCYCLOPAEDIA BRITANNICA

Now the oldest established encyclopaedia in print, the *Britannica* was founded in Edinburgh by Colin Macfarquhar and Andrew Bell and edited by William Smellie.

1775: FIRST MODERN FLUSHING TOILET

The basic principle of flushing human body waste away has been around since the Neolithic (the Skara Brae settlement had some such system and so did Vindolanda), but the first flushing toilet using the 'S' trap was invented by Edinburgh-born Alexander Cummings in 1775.

1775: US Navy

Kirkcudbright-born John Paul Jones (1747–92) became the first lieutenant of the American 'Continental Navy' and was known subsequently as 'the Father of the US Navy'.

1818: Chilean Navy

Lord Cochrane (see p. 97), one of the Royal Navy's great fighting captains, was hired by Bernardo O'Higgins to be the first commander of the Chilean navy. Cochrane is the model for both C. S. Forester's *Hornblower* and Patrick O'Brian's *Jack Aubrey*. Five Chilean ships have been named after him and Neruda wrote a poem on his life.

c.1820: Macadam

A type of smooth road construction invented by engineer John Loudon McAdam (1756–1836).

1823: Macintosh

Glaswegian chemist Charles Macintosh (1766–1843) patented his waterproof coat in 1823. Renowned as an innovative chemist, he became a Fellow of the Royal Society in 1824. The 'mac' underwent several refinements, most notably using vulcanized rubber in 1843.

1845: Pneumatic Rubber Tyre

The remarkable Stonehaven-born Robert William Thomson (1822–73) has been described, accurately enough, as 'Scotland's forgotten inventor'. Thomson invented many useful things, including the portable steam crane, as well as the rubber tyre, the now classic case of an invention ahead of its time. The tyre was reinvented in 1887 by another Scot, John Dunlop (1840–1921).

1847: ANAESTHETICS

A noted obstetrician who made several important advances in medicine, Sir James Simpson (1811–70) discovered the anaesthetic properties of chloroform in 1847. The medical profession was initially reluctant to accept Simpson's use of chloroform until 1853, when Queen Victoria had it while giving birth.

1848: KELVIN SCALE

Belfast-born Lord Kelvin (1824–1907) made many important scientific advances at Glasgow University, and devised the Kelvin temperature scale: the 'absolute thermometric scale'.

1859: FOGHORN

The first steam-power foghorn was installed in Nova Scotia by Glaswegian Robert Foulis (1796–1866).

1861: COLOUR PHOTOGRAPHY

The first permanent colour photograph was taken by Edinburgh-born James Clerk Maxwell (1831–79) – of a tartan ribbon. Maxwell, one of Scotland's greatest geniuses, has been described as the most important scientist after Newton and before Einstein.

1867: ANTISEPTICS

Born in Essex into a Quaker family, the surgeon Sir Joseph Lister (1827–1912) advocated and practised sterile surgery at Glasgow Royal Infirmary. Lister became one of humanity's greatest benefactors when he published his *Antiseptic Principle of the Practice of Surgery* (1867).

1876: MR WATSON IS TOLD TO 'COME HERE' ON THE TELEPHONE

The history of the invention of the telephone is horrendously controversial, but it seems that the first intelligible communication over the phone was from Edinburgh-born Alexander Graham Bell (1847–1922) to his assistant: 'Mr Watson, come here, I want to see you.'

1892: DIGESTIVE BISCUITS

These first appeared in 1892 in the biscuit range of the Edinburgh firm McVitie's. They were called 'digestive' because it was erroneously believed they had antacid properties.

1926: TELEVISION

John Logie Baird (1888–1946) succeeded in transmitting a human face on his 'televisor' and it's all been downhill from there.

1928: PENICILLIN

'When I woke up just after dawn on September 28, 1928, I certainly didn't plan to revolutionize all medicine by discovering the world's first antibiotic, or bacteria killer. But I guess that was exactly what I did.' Thus did Alexander Fleming (1881–1955) describe his accidental discovery of penicillin.

1996: FIRST CLONED MAMMAL

Including Dolly the Sheep in a list of 'inventions' may be seen as morally dubious – some agribusinesses describe themselves as in the business of 'manufacturing' food out of animals, after all – but the process by which Dolly came into being at Edinburgh's Roslin Institute is certainly an inventive one, using nuclear transfer to clone Dolly from a somatic cell. Dolly was named after Dolly Parton and died in 2003.

2012: Higgs Boson

I have read the Wikipedia article on the Higgs Boson and understand nothing, but whatever it is, it is named after Newcastle-born Peter Higgs, emeritus professor at the University of Edinburgh, who was awarded the Nobel Prize in Physics for his work at Edinburgh on subatomic particles.

2016: Gravitational Waves

Gravitational waves (see Wikipedia) are ripples in the curvature of the space–time continuum that generate as waves, a phenomenon predicted by Einstein in 1916 and confirmed in February 2016. Many institutions worldwide contributed to the discovery, and the University of Glasgow led the UK's contribution.